The
Pomeranian
Handbook

Sharon L. Vanderlip, D.V.M.

Filled with Full-color Photographs
Illustrations by Pam Tanzey

BARRON'S

About the Author

Sharon Vanderlip, D.V.M., has provided veterinary care to domestic and exotic animal species for more than twenty-five years. She has authored fifteen books on dog breeds and animal care and published numerous articles for scientific, veterinary, and general reading audiences.

Dr. Vanderlip served as clinical veterinarian for the University of California at San Diego School of Medicine, collaborated on research projects with the Zoological Society of San Diego, and is former chief of veterinary services for the National Aeronautics and Space Administration (NASA). Dr. Vanderlip is director of ICSB-San Diego, a practice that provides services in exotic and canine reproductive medicine and surgery. She has lectured worldwide on topics in canine and exotic animal medicine and is the recipient of various awards for her writing and dedication to animal health. She can be contacted at *www.sharonvanderlip.com*.

Acknowledgments

I would like to thank my husband, Jack Vanderlip, D.V.M., for his veterinary expertise in reviewing the final manuscript. Thanks to both my husband and our daughter, Jacquelynn Vanderlip, for taking care of everything at home so that I would have more time to write. And, of course, a big thank-you is extended to my editor, Kathleen Ganteaume.

Cover Credits

Front cover: Pets by Paulette, Isabelle Francais, Norvia Behling; Back cover: Pets by Paulette; Inside front cover: Cheryl Ertelt; Inside back cover: Pets by Paulette.

Photo Credits

Isabelle Francais: pages vi, 2, 3, 4, 6, 10, 20, 22, 23, 26, 35, 37, 41, 43, 47, 54, 58, 64, 66, 70, 71, 75, 83, 92, 99, 104, 109, 120, 123, 128, 135, 137, 142, 143, 145, 149, 150; Norvia Behling: 21, 28, 33, 36, 42, 45, 49 (top), 50, 56, 85, 87, 95, 98, 101, 107, 111, 115, 116, 125, 130, 144; Pets by Paulette: 5, 7, 11, 19, 38, 57, 89, 91, 96, 127, 138, 151; Cheryl Ertelt: 8, 18, 24, 55, 119, 141, 147; Shirley Fernandez: 49 (bottom), 53, 80, 105, 140; Tara Darling: 17, 74, 78.

© Copyright 2007 by Barron's Educational Series, Inc.

All inquiries should be addressed to:
Barron's Educational Series, Inc.
250 Wireless Boulevard
Hauppauge, New York 11788
http://www.barronseduc.com

ISBN-13: 978-0-7641-3545-3
ISBN-10: 0-7641-3545-7

Library of Congress Catalog Card No. 2006026222

Library of Congress Cataloging-in-Publication Data
Vanderlip, Sharon Lynn.
  The Pomeranian handbook / Sharon Vanderlip ;
  illustrations by Pam Tanzey.
      p. cm.
  Includes index.
  ISBN-13: 978-0-7641-3545-3
  ISBN-10: 0-7641-3545-7
  1. Pomeranian dog. I. Title.

SF429.P8V36 2007
636.76—dc22   2006012576

Printed in China
9 8 7 6 5 4 3 2 1

Important Note

This pet handbook gives advice to the reader on how to buy or adopt, and care for a Pomeranian. The author and publisher consider it important to point out that the advice given in this book applies to normally developed puppies or adult dogs acquired from recognized dog breeders or adoption sources, dogs that have been examined and are in excellent physical health with good temperament.

Anyone who adopts a fully grown dog should be aware that the animal has already formed its basic impressions of human beings and their customary actions. The new owner should watch the animal carefully, especially its attitude and behavior toward humans. If possible, the new owner should meet the previous owner before adopting the dog. If the dog comes from a shelter, the new owner should make an effort to obtain information about the dog's background, personality, and any individual peculiarities. Dogs coming from abusive homes or from homes in which they have been treated abnormally may react to handling in an unnatural manner, and they may have a tendency to snap or bite. Such dogs should only be adopted by people experienced with handling canine behavior problems.

Caution is further advised in the association of children with dogs, both puppies and adults, and in meeting other dogs, whether on or off leash.

Even well-behaved and carefully supervised dogs sometimes do damage to someone else's property or cause accidents. It is therefore in the owner's interest to be adequately insured against such eventualities, and we strongly urge all dog owners to purchase a liability policy that covers the dog.

Contents

Pomeranian ancestors were working dogs, guarding humans and herding sheep.

Chapter One

Pomeranian History: Proud, Prestigious, and Popular!

Pomeranian—thief of hearts! For more than a century Pomeranians have stolen the hearts of thousands of people. It's no wonder your heart has been captivated by this bright-eyed, beautiful, charismatic canine. Poms have graced the homes of high-society elite and palaces of royalty. A Pomeranian just might be a welcome addition to your home, too!

Pomeranians are very popular dogs indeed. According to registration statistics, out of 154 recognized American Kennel Club breeds, Poms ranked tenth in litter registrations and fourteenth in dog registrations in 2005.

So how did such a little dog take up such a big place in dog lovers' hearts? Pomeranians may be small in size, but they are giants when it comes to personality, spunk, and affection. Poms are bold, curious, outgoing, independent, and animated. They are extremely attractive, highly intelligent, heavily coated, and devoted. Poms make excellent watchdogs, bravely sounding warning barks at strangers. These courageous little action dogs want to investigate everything and participate in every activity.

Pomeranians are very sturdy dogs. It makes sense when you consider that they are credited with being descendants of large, powerful, hard working dogs known as Wolfspitz, or Wolfspitzen.

We do not know all the details of the Pomeranian's ancestral lineage, but what we do know is impressive. So let's take a journey through the Pomeranian's family album, from its early ancestry to present day. This little dog has a big story to tell!

The Very Beginning— Prehistoric Ancestors

There are hundreds of breeds of dogs, and every one of them, including the Pomeranian, can be traced to the same prehistoric carnivorous (meat-eating) relative, a creature

Dogs were first domesticated about 10,000 years ago.

America and is a distant descendant of Hesperocyonines.

About 7 million years ago, many canid species migrated from North America to Asia, possibly over a land bridge that may have existed at the time. These canids were not dogs as we know them today. No humans were there to record their migration or evolution, so we must rely on the fossil record. It tells us that, as difficult as it is to believe, the trunk of our Pomeranian's family tree originates with these wild, savage, primitive canines.

called Hesperocyonines. The fossil record tells us that Hesperocyonines evolved in North America about 40 million years ago and resembled a cross between a fox and a weasel. Hesperocyonines became extinct about 15 million years ago, but before its extinction, it gave rise to several canine species.

During the next several million years, many canine species evolved and then became extinct. A good example is the dire wolf (*Canis dirus*) that lived in North America during the Pleistocene era and died out as recently as 10,000 years ago. Fortunately, thirty-five species of canids managed to survive to the present day. These include foxes, wolves, coyotes, jackals, and dogs. Every one of these species evolved in North

Origin of the Breed—Nordic Roots

It is accepted as fact that wolves (*Canis lupus*) are the ancestors of today's dog breeds. Through selective breeding, dogs evolved from wolves and were first domesticated about 10,000 years ago. These dogs were wolflike in size, appearance, and behavior. Most historians agree that the forerunners of today's Pomeranian were large, powerful, working dogs from the Arctic regions of Iceland and Lapland. They were probably descendants of the northern European gray wolf. These dogs were commonly known as Spitz, Wolfspitz, or Wolfspitzen. Spitz is German for "sharp point," and the term was coined by the baron Count Eberhard

Pomeranians are Nordic to the core! They are sturdy, heavy-coated, miniature versions of their powerful, Wolfspitzen ancestors.

zu Sayne in the sixteenth century, presumably in reference to the refined, "foxy" features of the dog's nose and muzzle. Wolfspitz were large, muscular, heavily coated animals that were well adapted to a cold, harsh climate.

Wolfspitz-type dogs served humans in many ways. They were used for protection; guarding; herding cattle, sheep, and caribou; and pulling sledges. Descendants of the Wolfspitz eventually spread to different countries, where they were continually selected and bred according to size and working abilities to best suit the needs of humans. Through selective breeding, several different breeds were created, including the Pomeranian. Even today, these closely related dogs have retained and share many

instincts, behaviors, traits, and conformational characteristics.

Today's Pomeranian is a diminutive model of its ancestors. It has small,

Pomeranian Cousins

Descendants of the Wolfspitz include, but are not limited to, the Akita, Alaskan Malamute, Chow Chow, Finnish Spitz, German Spitzen, Keeshonden, Norwegian Elkhound, Samoyed, and Schipperke. The Pomeranian is considered to be a direct descendant of the German Spitzen group, which today comprises five different sizes of German Spitz breeds. The Pomeranian is believed to be a descendent of the smallest of the five German Spitz breeds.

erect ears deeply set in heavy fur to prevent them from freezing; a dense coat; and a tail covered with long, thick hair that curls over the back for added protection from the cold.

Royal Regard

Two queens influenced early Pomeranian history and popularity. In 1767, German-born Queen Charlotte, wife of King George III of England, brought two Pomeranians to England. The dogs, Phoebe and Mercury, reportedly came from an area near Pomerania. These dogs were depicted in paintings by the famous painter Sir Thomas Gainsborough, who is probably best known for his painting *The Blue Boy*. Gainsborough's paintings give us an excellent

Names, Places, and Record Keeping

How did the Pomeranian acquire its unusual name? It is believed that the first Pomeranian-type dogs became very popular more than two centuries ago, in what is now the northeast region of Germany, bordering the Baltic Sea. This area was known as Pomerania. Although the Pomeranian breed did not originate in Pomerania, this location is credited for selecting, breeding, and raising the ancestors of the breed and for creating the original Pomeranian type.

Pomerania has a long, complicated, and turbulent political history. Its borders and population underwent many changes throughout the centuries, and the area was devastated by wars. Under such conditions, dog-breeding records, if any were kept, would have been difficult to safeguard or maintain. Our most detailed written history of the early Pomeranian, therefore, starts with the breed's introduction to the United Kingdom, where it was first acknowledged as a true breed, the first Pomeranian breed club was established, and the first Pomeranian breed standard was written. The United Kingdom is also where Pomeranians were first formally exhibited—by the queen, no less!

DNA Genetic Testing Will Solve the Mystery!

Some people have suggested that the Pomeranian may have had early origins in other lands, with warmer climates, such as Egypt or Greece. These theories are based on ancient art that illustrates dogs with Pomeranian characteristics, such as a heavily frilled tail curled over the back, a thick coat, and erect ears.

It will not be long before the Pomeranian's exact line of descent can be accurately confirmed. Scientists have already mapped out the dog's genome (genetic makeup), and DNA testing of many canine breeds to identify their true origins has already been completed and published. Given the Pomeranian's enormous popularity, DNA testing for this presumed Spitz is just around the corner!

idea of what Poms looked like 200 years ago. In these paintings we see a much larger version of today's Pomeranian, reportedly weighing as much as 30 to 50 pounds (13.5—22.5 kg), but still sporting the heavy coat, erect ears (larger than today's Pom's ears), and a tail curled over the back. Two of Gainsborough's more well-known paintings of Pomeranians are *Pomeranian Bitch with Pups* and *Mrs. Robinson with Pomeranian.*

From the Arctic regions to your backyard garden, your Pomeranian's history spans thousands of miles and thousands of years.

Two generations and a century later, Victoria, who was Queen Charlotte's granddaughter, also developed a passion for Poms. We have the benefit of illustrations and descriptions found in early books written during Queen Victoria's time, such as Vero Shaw's *The Illustrated Book of the Dog* (1880) to give us a good idea of what most Poms looked like at the end of the nineteenth century. The illustrations in Shaw's book titled *A Black Pomeranian* and *Pomeranian "Charly"* and *Maltese "Hugh"* show us Pomeranians close in type to today's Poms. ("Charly," by the way, is a white Pom.) Based on other animals and objects in the illustrations, the Pomeranians in Shaw's illustrations appear to weigh at least 25 pounds (11 kg).

Pomeranians are recognized worldwide for their charismatic "smile."

Across the English Channel, in France, the Pomeranian continued to win the hearts of the ruling class. Josephine Tascher de la Pagerie, wife of the French emperor Napoleon, was enamored with the little dogs and housed several at her home, Château Malmaison.

The royal passion for Poms was not limited to women, however. Queen Charlotte's grandson King George IV also owned a black-and-white Pom. Nevertheless, it is Queen Victoria who is most responsible for promoting the Pomeranian and bringing it to the public's attention. It is reported that she imported several Pomeranians from Italy in 1888 and established a large breeding kennel

for them. One of Queen Victoria's favorite Pomeranians from Italy was a red sable she named Windsor's Marco. He was comparatively small for the breed and a little different in type from that known in England at the time. It is interesting to speculate about Marco's Italian pedigree and how it contributed to his unusually small size—a lightweight for the time—only twelve pounds (5.45 kg)!

Importing smaller Poms from Italy apparently worked out well for Queen Victoria's breeding program. She is credited with reducing the size of her Poms by 50 percent, from 30 pounds to 15 pounds (13.5 to 7 kg), during her lifetime.

Small, Smaller, Smallest

When Queen Victoria exhibited Marco in 1891, his small size piqued a lot of interest, and smaller-sized Pomeranians were immediately the rage. Breeders began selecting smaller specimens for breeding.

This raises the question of how a breed that originally weighed up to 50 pounds (22.5 kg) could be scaled down to one-tenth its original size in such a short time. Historians report that this was accomplished by consistently breeding the smallest animals to the smallest animals. This would have been risky business, because breeders had to distinguish runts and dwarfism from individuals that were healthy but simply smaller in size. It also required breeding techniques such as line-breeding (breeding related animals, such as cousins) and inbreeding (breeding very closely related animals, such as a father-daughter breeding or a brother-sister breeding). Inbreeding is the fastest way to set specific traits, good and bad, within a breed. Inbreeding is not without risks and as a result, some of the early Poms had problems, including excessively domed skulls.

To develop sturdy, genetically sound lines of Pomeranians, breeders of the late 1800s had to select small dogs in good health, with the desired qualities and characteristics of the breed. This was quite a challenge, but today's Pom is proof of success: Of all the toy breeds, the Pomeranian is arguably the hardiest one with the fewest medical problems.

Shows, Clubs, and Standards

In 1891, fourteen Poms were exhibited at a dog show in England. Among them were Queen Victoria's own dogs. The queen had many different-colored Poms, and it is said that special color classes were sometimes created just to accommodate her uncommon color varieties. Because all things royal were also quite fashionable, the queen's affection for Pomeranians captured the

Charm to spare! It is no wonder that Pomeranians consistently rank among the most popular breeds in the world.

public's attention and imagination. Pomeranians soared in popularity as elite and fashionable pets and sold for exorbitant sums.

In England in 1891 the Pomeranian Club was established and wrote the first Pomeranian breed standard. Ten years later, more than fifty Poms competed in shows, and five years after that the number of entries doubled. By that time, the personable Pomeranian had captured the hearts and imaginations of dog fanciers around the world.

Welcome to America!

As news of the endearing toy breed spread throughout the world, so did its popularity. At some time in the 1800s, a Pom set paws in the United States

for the first time and in 1898 the first Pom, named Dick, was recorded by the American Kennel Club (AKC). No one could have guessed how very many more would soon cross the Atlantic!

In 1900 the Pomeranian breed was recognized by the AKC and the American Pomeranian Club (APC) was formed. In the same year, a Pomeranian named Nubian Rebel was given the prestigious award of Best in Breed at a dog show. Not surprisingly, this famous little dog later went on to earn his championship title.

The AKC welcomed the APC as a member club in 1909, and the first Pomeranian specialty show quickly followed in 1910, with 138 dogs competing—an impressive entry number for a breed so recently introduced to the United States. This was only the beginning of a long success story. By 1926, a Pomeranian by the name of Glen Rose Flashaway won its group title at the venerable Westminster Kennel Club, and from then on, the Pom's success in the show ring and its popularity as a companion only continued to soar. The Pomeranian population grew steadily, and for a decade this perky little dog ranked among the top ten favorite breeds in the United States. At the time of this writing, Poms are ranked fourteenth of 154 AKC-recognized breeds.

Chapter Two
Pomeranian Perfection

If you were to design the perfect little dog, what would it be? Why, a Pomeranian, of course! Poms are beautiful and bold. They are also a nice, portable size, yet willing and able to cover the ground on their own. They are devoted companions, brave guardians, and strong for their size. Poms are full of personality, eager to please, and love to show off. They make for tough competition at dog shows and events. Whether in conformation, agility, or obedience classes, Poms have a natural way of stealing the show!

These bright-eyed canines are affectionate, but they are also independent. Pomeranians have minds of their own and use them well. Poms are quick learners, so it's no wonder they have earned a wide variety of titles and awards, ranging from championships to obedience titles, and from Canine Good Citizenship certificates to Hall of Fame awards.

The Pomeranian Breed Standard

Specific guidelines, called the Pomeranian breed standard, describe the ideal Pom. This is the type of Pom breeders strive to produce and the type that judges select as their winners. The Pomeranian breed standard has changed slightly over the years, particularly as it relates to size, but for the most part, the standard has remained consistent.

Small in Size, Big on Balance

The first breed standard was written in 1891, the same year the first Pomeranian Club was established in the United Kingdom. The standard categorized Pomeranians into two groups: more than 8 pounds (3.6 kg) and less than 8 pounds.

The smaller-sized Pom was so popular that in 1894, at Crufts dog show, the standard was revised to create a toy category for Poms less than 7 pounds (3.18 kg). This made a total of three Pomeranian size categories for the show ring: small Poms weighing less than 7 pounds, and larger Poms weighing more than 16 pounds (7.2 kg), or Poms weighing between 7 and 16 pounds.

Today in the United Kingdom, the Pomeranian standard calls for males

The ideal Pomeranian is well balanced, sturdy, and has a beautiful coat.

to weigh 4 to 4.5 pounds (1.8 to 2 kg) and females from 4.5 to 5.5 pounds (2.5 kg). In the United States, Pomeranians range from 3 to 7 pounds (1.36 kg to 3.18 kg), and the ideal weight for the show ring is considered 4 to 6 pounds (1.8 to 2.7 kg).

The most important thing about Pomeranian size is that the animal should be balanced overall in quality. Substance, health, and personality should never be sacrificed for small size. A Pom that is weak in conformation, or deficient in physical or mental makeup, is not characteristic of the breed. Pomeranians should be small, but they should also always be sturdy,

moderately muscled dogs, reminiscent of their Arctic ancestors.

Interpreting the Standard

The Pomeranian breed standard details how the perfect Pomeranian should look, move, and behave. If you are thinking of raising, exhibiting, or training Poms, then you will refer to this valuable guide frequently. If you simply want to learn the very essence of what makes a Pom a Pom, understanding the breed standard is the best place to start!

Quality and Character Above All

The Pomeranian breed standard emphasizes that overall quality is more important than size. Although Pomeranians are small, they are medium-boned dogs that look and feel solid and sturdy. The Pom's overall appearance is one of a compact dog. It is short backed and heavy coated, with a high-set tail that lies flat on the back.

Strong character and personality are essential in Poms. The standard uses words such as *animated, alert, active, inquisitive, intelligent*, and *vivacious* to describe this happy, bold extrovert. A Pom's general attitude should reflect all of these traits, and the standard says that Poms are "cocky" and "commanding." You only have to meet a Pomeranian once to know exactly what the standard means!

Pomeranians should also be sound. This means good, solid, flowing, balanced movement with good reach in the forequarters and lots of drive from the hindquarters. This is to be expected from a moderately muscled and well-balanced dog. The rear legs move in line with the front legs on the same side. This does not mean that Poms pace. It means that if a line were drawn illustrating the pathway of the front legs, the hind legs would follow that line precisely. When Poms gait out, they balance movement with the opposite feet. That is, the left front foot moves with the right rear foot and the right front foot moves with the left rear

Pomeranians are intelligent and learn quickly. A well-mannered Pom is a joy to own.

foot. Poms should not be cowhocked. Cowhocks are unattractive and restrict action and freedom of movement. Obviously, a sound Pom shows no signs of limping or lameness.

The Pom is recognized for its profuse double coat, consisting of a very dense, soft undercoat and a thick, coarser-textured outer coat. The undercoat insulates against the cold and the outer coat protects against harsh weather, such as rain and snow. This is exactly the type of coat one would expect from a breed originating in the far northern regions. The coat is heavy and full on the neck, shoulders, chest, back, and sides. It is compact and shorter on the head and legs.

Know the Breed Standard's Terminology

Terminology	Definition
Brisket	Breast bone, sternum
Cowhock	Hocks turn inward
Dewclaws	Front dewclaws are the underdeveloped, first metacarpal bone on the front feet, on the upper inside of the pastern. Hind dewclaws, also called spurs or wolf's claws, are not always present in Poms. They are the first metatarsal bones of each foot, on the inner surface of the rear pasterns. They may be surgically removed.
Gait	Type of movement. A correct gait requires correct anatomical construction. To achieve balance while gaiting, a Pom's legs converge slightly inward toward a center line underneath its body.
Hock	Joint on hind leg, between lower thigh and rear pastern
Lippy	Lips are too large, too lax, or there is too much redundant lip tissue, and the lips are overhung or pendulous (for example, some hounds are "lippy").
Open Fontanelle	A "soft spot," or area on the skull where ossification or bone closure is not complete.
Overshot	The upper jaw extends beyond the lower jaw.
Pasterns	The metacarpus, the area between the carpus (wrist) and the foot. Pom pasterns are straight and strong.
Plume, plumed tail	Long hairs in the shape of a plume
Points	Areas of color on the face restricted to the eyebrows, inside of ears, muzzle, back, of thighs, legs, feet
Snipey	A foreface or muzzle that is too weak, fine, narrow, or pointed. *Snipey* may also mean the dog lacks sufficient underjaw.
Stifle	Hind limb knee joint, where upper and lower thighs articulate. Pom stifles are moderately bent, or angulated, and well defined
Stop	The stop is situated between the eyes, at the junction of the frontal bones of the skull and the bones of the upper jaw (maxilla). It is the area where the muzzle meets the foreface.
Undershot	The lower jaw is longer than the upper jaw, also called *inferior prognasthism*.
Withers	This is where the height of a dog is measured. It is the area at the base of the neck where it joins the back. It is the union between the upper part of the shoulder blade and the spinous processes of the first and second thoracic vertebrae (spine).

Correct Head and Skull Type

Pomeranians must have the right type of head, correctly shaped and complete with a beautiful face. Eyes are an important part of a Pom's expression. They should be bright, dark, correctly placed, medium sized, almond shaped, and set well into the skull. Small ears are placed high on the skull and carried erect.

The head should be properly balanced in relation to the body. Poms have short, straight, fine muzzles, and their faces look somewhat "foxlike." This should not be confused with being snipey. Poms should never be snipey or lippy.

When viewed from the side, the Pomeranian's skull should have a wedge shape to it, reminiscent of its Spitz family. The wedge can be visualized by drawing and connecting imaginary lines from the tip of the nose up through the center of the eyes and the tips of the ears.

The Pomeranian has a well-defined stop. Teeth are an important component of the overall makeup of the Pom's skull and jaws. The teeth should meet in proper alignment, called a "scissors" bite. In this dental arrangement, the outer surfaces of the lower incisor (front) teeth engage with the inner surfaces of the upper incisors when the mouth is closed. This requires the jaws to be of equal length and the teeth to erupt at 90-degree angles from the jaws. The standard is a bit flexible in that it does allow for

Pomeranians should have excellent skeletal structure, including a correct, rounded skull with a well-defined stop. The head is carried high and the body should be well-balanced and sturdy.

one misaligned tooth. Otherwise, the mouth should not be undershot or overshot. These jaw abnormalities are undesirable in Poms and can cause dental problems.

A correct Pom skull is slightly rounded and *closed*. It is not domed. Skulls in which the bones have not completely closed on top (leaving a "soft spot," or open fontanelle), or skulls that are domed, can be an indication of genetic or medical problems.

Body Conformation

The Pom's neck is short, and its head is carried high and proudly. Shoulders and limbs are moderately muscled and the back is short. The standard calls for a level "topline." A topline is normally considered the dog's entire upper outline seen in

The Pomeranian Kaleidoscope of Colors

Coat Color	Description
All other colors	All colors are acceptable, including any other color not described in this chart.
Black	Deep, dark black outer coat; undercoat may be slightly lighter shade of black; no other colors present in the coat.
Blue	Color ranges from light gray to deep, dark gray. The undercoat is silver gray and the outer coat has a dark blue-gray hue that may seem black until compared with a true black Pom. Blues are silver at birth and darken to almost a black color as they mature. By adulthood they usually have a dark blue-gray outer coat.
Brindle	Base color gold, red, or orange
Brown	Pure brown, ranging from light chocolate to a deep, dark, intense brown. A diluted brown coloration is known as *beaver* or *biscuit*. No black tipping, or shading, or other colors should be present in the coat of genetically brown Poms.
Cream	Pale yellow outer coat can appear darker than undercoat, no white
Orange	Ranges from light creamy orange to deep, dark orange
Red	Deep rust red
Shaded sables	Shaded sables: shaded coats with three or more colors, guard hairs are darker at the tips. • Blue sable: light blue undercoat, dark blue outer coat with black-tipped guard hairs • Brown sable: light brown undercoat, darker brown outer coat, black-tipped guard hairs • Cream sable: very pale undercoat, light yellow outer coat, black-tipped guard hairs • Orange sable: light orange or cream undercoat, orange outer coat, guard hairs are dark red at the tips • Red sable: pale red/orange undercoat, dark red outer coat, black-tipped guard hairs • Wolf sable: light gray undercoat, with dark, steel gray outer coat, black-tipped guard hairs

Color of eyelid margins, nose, lips, foot pads	Pattern
Consistent with base color	
Black	
Gray to light black, also called *blue*	
Thin or wide black cross stripes over base color. The striping may extend completely or partially over the body. Brindle pattern may occur together with other coat patterns, such as tan markings or parti-color.	Consistent with base color
Brown for true brown Poms. Light brown to beige for dilute brown Poms.	
Black	
Black	
Black	
Preferably black	

The Pomeranian Kaleidoscope of Colors (continued)

Coat Color	Description
Tan Pattern	Color varies: light cream, tan, deep rust, dark mahogany Black and tan: deep, dark tan coloration preferred Blue and tan: depth of tan coloration to be consistent with depth of coloration of blue coat Chocolate/brown and tan: depth of tan coloration to be consistent with depth of coloration of brown coat
White	White undercoat, white outer coat, no other colors present. White was one of the more common colors of the early Pomeranians.
Parti-color	White with any other color distributed in patches. A white blaze on the head is preferred.

profile, from the ears to the tail. For example, in contrast to the level topline of a Pomeranian, a German Shepherd has a sloping topline. The Pom's plumed tail is set high and lies flat and straight on the back. It spreads out to appear to be a smooth part of the topline. It should not look like the curled tail of its ancestors. A true topline may not be obvious to the beginner. It is easy to be distracted by the plumed tail and thick coat, especially if the animal's coat and tail have been groomed in such a way as to hide or enhance certain aspects of its conformation. This is one good reason to always feel the dog's body, to make sure it is balanced and strong and that the perceived outline is the true outline.

The distance from the Pom's point of the shoulder to its point of the buttock is slightly less than the distance from the withers to the ground. The distance from the brisket to the ground is half the distance from the floor to the withers. The upper foreleg and the shoulder blade are equal in length. The distance from the elbows to the withers is about the same distance as from the ground to the elbow. The thighs are moderately muscled, stifles are slightly bent, and hocks are perpendicular to the ground. All of these body parts are balanced on straight, strong pasterns set on arched, compact feet.

Coat Quality

Pomeranians have a heavy double coat. The undercoat is soft and dense. The outer coat is long, straight, glossy, yet harsh textured. The dense undercoat allows the abundant outer coat to stand up and out from the body. The coat is particularly profuse from the neck to the shoulders and chest, forming a large frill. The coat is short and dense on the head. The

Color of eyelid margins, nose, lips, foot pads	Pattern
	Above each eye, sides of muzzle, cheeks, inside ears, chest above fore-limbs (one spot or two "rosettes"), legs, feet, sometimes a thin line of tan along top of each toe, under tail, and hair on back of thighs
Pink at birth, pigmenting to black by adulthood	
Consistent with base color	

Canine Mona Lisa

One of the most endearing and unique features of a Pomeranian is the way its face, mouth, and lips combine to form a sweet, yet subtle, canine "smile."

front and rear legs have long hair, especially on the posterior aspects, known as *feathers* or *feathering*.

Coats of Many Colors

One of the most alluring aspects of the Pomeranian breed, and one that is very important for winning in the show ring, is its thick, luxurious, profuse coat. The Pomeranian is famous for its dense, beautiful coat, accentuated by its high-set, heavily plumed tail resting flat against its back. The Pomeranian's beautiful coat and tail require good

A Pomeranian carries its head high and proudly. Poms should have a level topline.

nutrition and regular care and grooming to prevent matting and to keep the skin healthy and the hair lustrous (see "Feeding Your Pomeranian" and "Grooming Your Pomeranian").

With so many colors from which to choose, you may decide to own more than one Pom!

American Kennel Club Group Classifications

Group I	Sporting Dogs
Group II	Hounds
Group III	Working Dogs
Group IV	Terriers
Group V	Toys
Group VI	Non-Sporting Dogs
Group VII	Herding Dogs
Miscellaneous Class	

Pomeranians come in a wide variety of colors. The American Kennel Club allows all colors, patterns, and variations to be exhibited, without preference for one over the other. The overall quality, health, and temperament of the dog are much more important than its color. Successful breeders must known their animals well and have a good understanding of genetics, as well as coat color inheritance, to meet the challenges of breeding the best dogs possible in the purest, most attractive colors.

Color Classes at the Pomeranian Specialty Shows

The Open Classes at specialty shows are divided by color: red, orange, cream, and sable; black, brown, and blue; and any other color, pattern, or variation.

Are you ready to add a little color to your life? The Pomeranian has one of the largest color selections of any breed. Picking a favorite color will not be easy!

No matter what color you prefer, remember that health and personality are much more important than color.

Group V: Toys

Affenpinscher	Miniature Pinscher
Brussels Griffon	Papillon
Chihuahua	Pekingese
Chinese Crested	**Pomeranian**
English Toy Spaniel	Poodle (Toy)
Italian Greyhound	Pug
Japanese Chin	Shih Tzu
Maltese	Silky Terrier
Manchester Terrier (Toy)	Yorkshire Terrier

Pomeranians come in a wide variety of colors and all colors are accepted in the show ring. Health, conformation, and character are always more important than color.

Never buy a Pomeranian based on color alone or as a first consideration.

The Pomeranian's Place in the Dog World

The Pomeranian is a member of the Toy Group: AKC classification Group V.

You have studied Pomeranians, learned the standard, memorized the coat colors, and remembered the show and group classifications. But you have only just begun! The best way to learn about Poms is to go out and see them in person, speak to their breeders, and interact directly with these charming canines. It is time to start thinking about how a Pom will fit into your life and how to find the best match for you, so let's get started!

Chapter Three

Considerations Before You Buy

The Perfect Pom— Is It the Perfect Dog for *You*?

You meet a Pomeranian for the first time and fall helplessly in love with its outgoing personality and overall beauty. This confident canine is no stranger to admirers. Its endearing appearance, portable size, alert countenance, and luxurious coat have made the Pomeranian a favorite among dog lovers worldwide and set it apart from all other dog breeds.

Your heart tells you a Pomeranian *must* become part of your life *right now*. But good judgment and common sense remind you that owning and caring for a dog means a lot of responsibility. Such an important decision and long-term commitment deserves serious thought before deciding whether a Pom is the right match for you. So here are some important things to consider.

Tender Companion, Tough Competitor

There is a lot to learn about Pomeranians and their care. Pomeranians want to have everything both ways. They want to be with the people they love and they want their independence. They love to be carried and snuggled, but they really are not "lap dogs" in the way many toy breeds are. Poms are active and curious. They

It's easy to fall in love with a Pom, especially a Pom puppy! Don't be an impulse buyer. Pom ownership is a big responsibility. Make sure the time is right and that a Pom is the right dog for you.

prefer to run about freely on their own and explore. Poms are devoted and protective of their owners, yet they can be wary or suspicious of strangers. Pomeranians are vivacious, but they need peace and quiet and a private space to themselves. They are intelligent, quick learners and easy to train, but if they become bored with lessons or games, Poms can be a bit stubborn about cooperating. Poms are down-to-earth dogs that love human companionship, and yet, they are often proud, sassy, and arrogant. Pomeranians are happy and social, but when it comes to dog show events, they are tough competitors. They are little dogs that do not know they are little! As descendants of powerful, hardworking dogs, Poms are sturdy, active, and energetic. These bold little dogs consider themselves as big and tough as any other dog, and they will not back down when challenged or confronted. Poms may be tiny, but they are giants when it comes to courage, enthusiasm, energy, and intelligence.

Poms are loving companions but they can be mischievous and are full of energy. Be prepared!

Toy Sized and Energized

Do not let that small size fool you! When it comes to Poms, *small* is synonymous with *animated*. Poms are not sedentary pets that sit around on cushions all day long looking like decorative toys.

Toy size does not imply that Pomeranians are cheap to care for, feed, or house, either. Like all dogs, Pomeranians need high-quality nutri-tion to keep them in excellent health throughout life, from puppyhood to old age. Active Poms must have high-quality calories to support their high-energy activities. Excellent nutri-tion helps Poms to grow and maintain their gorgeous coats. Of course, regular grooming is also a must, and this requires patience, time, skill, and materials—or the funds to hire a groomer.

Pomeranians are inquisitive and adventurous. If you do not find things to entertain your little dog, she will find her own form of entertainment, including digging in the garden or under the fence, chewing, barking, and exploring. Make plans for a well-fenced yard for exercise, doors that close and latch securely, safe indoor housing, plenty of toys and activities, and lots of time

Poms hate to be bored. Make sure you give your Pom lots of exercise and toys.

to exercise, socialize, train, and groom this dynamic canine. And expect sudden bursts of energy. Poms may look like fancy, plush toys, but they are mobile vortexes much of the time. Be forewarned and be prepared!

Socialization and Training

Pomeranians are fun to train, but because they are so smart and such quick learners, they can be challenging. The best way to train your Pom to do what you want her to do, or to behave appropriately, is to make her *want* to cooperate (see "The Performance Pomeranian: Training Your Pomeranian"). Plan on spending the time required to teach your little Spitz the basics. Keep in mind that lessons need repeating and that several short training sessions are better than one long one.

Socialization is the first step to training and is a very important part of Pomeranian personality, life, and happiness. Socialization starts at puppyhood and continues throughout life. As the standard tells us, Pomeranian character is a very important aspect of the breed. Much of a Pom's personality is determined by the type and amount of socialization it receives. Between three and nine weeks of age, socialization is extremely important for Pom puppies to ensure that they develop strong characters and are not shy or fearful.

Many Pomeranians have earned championship titles and various awards. With a little bit of luck and a lot of hard work, your Pom can join their ranks. After all, she's definitely smart enough to go far beyond the basics. Poms are fierce competitors, and your Pom's successes in any endeavors are the result of your time, effort, patience, and skills combined with her natural, physical, and intellectual abilities. Winning is a team effort!

Poms must receive lots of love, attention, handling, and training throughout their entire lives. All of these require a lot of time and dedication. Pomeranians come by their high activity level naturally. It is an ingrained part of their genetic makeup, inherited from their working ancestors. If you are considering owning a Pom, plan on being very busy. She will be a constant companion and a friend—for life—and that's a long time! Pomeranians have been known to live into their late teens.

So, can you make the commitment? Do you have enough time, space, and finances for this charismatic canine?

Home Sweet Home

Your small companion's ancestors may have enjoyed roughing it in the great outdoors and living in snow dens, but your Pom needs a more comfortable lifestyle. She needs a place to sleep, excellent care, good food, and a loving family.

Today's Pomeranian is a house pet. Pomeranians need protection from very hot weather and should not

A Pomeranian's personality and character are greatly influenced by the type and amount of socialization it receives, especially between three and nine weeks of age.

be exposed to temperature extremes. Pomeranians need good ventilation, fresh air, and a cool, protected area.

Exercise

All dogs require daily exercise, and the Pomeranian is no exception. Even though Pomeranians are small, they need adequate space to run around and exercise. A daily walk on a leash, or a romp in the yard, will help keep your companion physically fit and in good health. Always be present to supervise and exercise your Pom. Play games with her and make sure she does not escape from the yard. Never leave your Pomeranian unsupervised in the backyard and whatever you do, *never leave your pet alone outside or tied to a tree, a post, or a line in the backyard.*

Pomeranians need daily exercise. Never leave your Pom alone outside or tied to a tree or post in the backyard. Supervise your Pom at all times.

Outdoor play means additional work grooming out tangles, burrs, grass awns, dirt, parasites, and mats, so be ready to brush your Pom after every outdoor adventure.

A Profuse Coat

Pomeranians have a lot of hair! The coat is thick and long and needs regular grooming. Set aside time for grooming sessions (see "Grooming Your Pomeranian") to keep your Pom's skin and coat healthy.

All dogs shed sometime during the year. If you groom your Pom at least once a week, and ideally once daily, shedding should not be too bothersome. Most of the shed and broken hairs will end up in the hairbrush and not on your clothing or furniture.

A well-groomed Pomeranian is stunning and attracts admirers like a magnet. Just wait until you go for a walk with your pet. It will seem like your Pomeranian is "on parade"!

The Commitment

Bringing a new dog into your life is a major decision. Dog ownership is both a joy and a serious responsibility. During the years, your Pomeranian will rely on you for affection, attention, good nutrition, grooming, exercise, training, and excellent health care. To satisfy these needs, you must be prepared for the financial aspects of responsible dog ownership, as well as for the investments you cannot really measure: time and emotion. When you bring a Pom into your life, you are making a promise to her that you will care for her all of her life. In return, your Pom will give you a gift you cannot buy: many years of friendship, happiness, and devotion. It is a wonderful unspoken agreement of love between you and your canine companion.

The Best Time to Acquire a Pomeranian

Your heart is set on a Pomeranian and your decision is made. So when is the best time to introduce a Pomeranian into your life and your home? You may want a Pomeranian right now, but there may be other cir-

A Quick Quiz

Every Pomeranian has its own unique personality, but there are distinct behavioral and inherited (genetic) traits distinctive to the breed—traits that are deeply ingrained in these animated little dogs. The characteristics that have made the Pomeranian a treasured pet of royalty and the elite are the same traits that make the Pom a precious and desirable companion today. They include intelligence, an alert and outgoing personality, a beautiful coat, and an affectionate nature. Poms do not like to be left alone at home. Your Pom will want to be with you every chance she can. She will demand your full attention. If you are planning on bringing a Pomeranian into your life, be sure you have a lot of time to spend with her!

Here's a little quiz to help you determine if a Pomeranian is the right dog for you.

1. Do you enjoy the company of a small dog that is beautiful, arrogant, and bold?

2. Are you looking for a dog that is intelligent, affectionate, and active?

3. Do you have a lot of time and love to give a little dog that craves attention, loves pampering, and wants to be part of every family activity?

4. Can you afford to feed your Pom high-quality nutrition and provide her with veterinary care?

5. Will you have time to exercise your Pom every day?

6. Do you have time to groom your Pom regularly, or can you afford to pay a professional groomer to do the job?

7. Do you have the time and patience to train your companion?

If you have answered yes to these questions, then you just might be ready to join the ranks of thousands of people who have owned and loved Pomeranians!

cumstances that prevent you from fulfilling this dream immediately.

First you must start by finding the perfect Pom. This is easier said than done. Good Poms are not always immediately available. Start contacting breeders far in advance of when you expect to buy a Pom, so you can visit them and be placed on a waiting list. It is hard to be patient, but in the end you will find a Pomeranian that is ideal for you. It will be worth the wait and you will not be disappointed.

If you have too many obligations and you have very little free time, postpone your purchase until you have the time to give your Pomeranian the care and attention she deserves. Pomeranians thrive on company and affection. If you do not have enough time to spend with your little dog, she will become bored and unhappy when left all alone, especially if left for long periods of time. Lonely dogs and puppies often get into mischief, and that's when good dogs turn bad. If your Pom has nothing to do and you are not there to keep her company, she can develop

Poms require a lot of care and attention and they have long life spans. Be sure you have time for a Pom—not just now, but for the next several years—before you bring one home.

unwanted behaviors, including chewing, digging, destroying objects, trying to escape, and incessant barking or yapping.

If you are moving or changing jobs, adding a new pet to your life will probably add more stress than enjoyment. If you are planning a vacation soon, wait until after you return from your travels so you do not have to make arrangements for animal care in your absence. A change in environment, caregivers, schedules, or diet can be very stressful for a dog, especially a puppy.

Never buy a puppy as a gift for someone else. Pet ownership is a responsibility not everyone wants to assume. People who want a pet also want to choose it themselves. After all, selecting a pet is a big part of the fun and important in determining whether the animal is a suitable match.

Do not buy a Pomeranian during the holiday season. Holidays are times when most people already have too much to do with visitors and commitments. New pets often are overlooked in the busy holiday shuffle with all the distractions and excitement. Families cannot take the time out during the holidays to learn about, supervise, socialize, and care for a new animal. Visitors and guests may stress, frighten, or mishandle the new arrival. They may even be bitten. Someone may forget to close a door or a gate and your new Pomeranian may escape, be lost or injured, or even be killed by a moving vehicle. In the holiday confusion, your Pom could miss a meal, or be overfed, unless someone is specifically assigned the responsibility of feeding. Finally, dogs purchased and transported during the holidays are more stressed and prone to illness than usual. Pomeranians transported in cold weather over long distances can suffer and die from hypothermia (low body temperature), hypoglycemia (low blood sugar), and dehydration. To prevent stress to yourself and to your new canine companion, wait until the holidays are over before you bring your Pom home.

For the safety of all of your pets, keep your Pom separated from the others until you know how they will behave together. Never leave your pets alone together unsupervised until you are absolutely positive you can trust them!

Household Pets and Your Pom

Your Pomeranian (we will call her Charm) is full of energy and curiosity. She has a keen sense of smell and is interested in meeting all the new members of your family, including other household pets. Make sure the introductions are done slowly and safely. For example, if you own another dog or a cat, do not expect them to be friends at the onset. Your other pets will be cautious and possibly jealous of the newcomer. A resentful cat can inflict serious injury on an unsuspecting dog, especially a tiny puppy. Eye injuries from cat scratches are common accidents suffered by dogs. And if you have another dog in the home, remember that it may be jealous of the attention you are giving Charm, particularly if it is an adult or aged animal. Even if your pets are happy to have Charm join the family, be sure that they do not play too roughly and accidentally injure her. Pomeranians are

sturdy little dogs, but they are still small and easily knocked over or hurt by larger dogs. A tiny Pom puppy can very easily be injured.

A good way to start introductions in the family is to place Charm in a safe area of the home where you can observe her closely and where she can watch and smell the other animals and they cannot reach her. For example, if you have a laundry area, or space next to the kitchen, you can place a barrier to prevent Charm from running loose in the house without your permission until she adapts to her new environment and your other pets are used to her. Make sure the barrier has mesh small enough to prevent escape or accidental injury and that Charm cannot become trapped in it. There are several types of wire cage pens with solid pan floors designed for toy breed dogs. You may put Charm in one of these pens or in her travel ken-

Gradually introduce your Pom to your other pets. Supervise them closely until you know they are compatible.

nel or crate for the first few evenings so that your other household pets can approach and investigate, but cannot frighten or harm her.

Remember to pay extra attention to your established pets so they are not jealous. It will be a real challenge juggling your attentions among your pets and spreading your affection so that they all feel they have received their fair share, especially if your other pets are also Pomeranians! Poms can be very jealous and possessive.

In most cases, animals learn to live together peacefully in a household. In the unlikely situation one of your dogs is aggressive, neutering (spaying or castrating) may improve the situation. For best results, pets should be neutered at a young age.

In addition to looking out for Charm's safety, you must protect the safety of your tinier and more vulnerable pets as well. These include mice, rats, hamsters, guinea pigs, rabbits, ferrets, birds, and reptiles. Pomeranians are not hunters, but back in the recesses of their minds are the instincts of primitive ancestors. Charm may have the notion that these small animals are fair game, or she may simply consider them interesting toys. In spite of her small size, Charm can play roughly with tiny pets. Small pets and birds sense when a dog is in the area and will be frightened and stressed if their cage is approached. Pomeranians are clever and quick! Make sure the lid or door to your small pet's cage is securely fastened. Then place the cage where Charm cannot access it. Remember, she has a good sense of smell and will easily find these animals, so do not just place them out of sight—*place them out of reach* until you are absolutely certain everyone gets along well. *Never leave your pets together unsupervised!*

Good Reasons to Neuter Your Pomeranian

It might sound surprising, but neutering is a form of good preventive veterinary care. In fact, neutering your Pom is one of the most important health decisions you will make.

The neutering procedure is called *gonadectomy* and refers to the inactivation or removal of some, or all, of the tissues in the body associated with reproduction: testicles in the male, and ovaries and uterus in the female. Removal of the testicles is called *castration*. Removal of the ovaries and uterus is called a *spay*, or more technically, an *ovariohysterectomy*, or OVH.

Female Pomeranians usually come into estrus (also called *in heat* or *in season*) around the age of six months and cycle approximately every six months thereafter, depending on their family genetics. Ideally, females should be spayed before their first estrous cycle, and certainly before the second estrous cycle. Spaying Charm before her first estrous cycle will significantly reduce her chances of developing mammary (breast) cancer later in life. If you wait until after her second estrous cycle, Charm will have almost as much chance of developing breast cancer than if she had not been spayed. Mammary cancer is common in older dogs, and 50 percent of mammary cancer in dogs is malignant, or life threatening. So it makes good medical sense to spay Charm at a young age.

Early surgical neutering can be performed safely on Pomeranians between sixteen and twenty weeks of age. Studies have shown that prepubertal gonadectomy (neutering before sexual maturity is reached) does not affect growth rate, food intake, or weight gain of growing dogs. In 1993 the American Veterinary Medical Association formally approved early neutering of dogs and cats.

Health Advantages

There are many health advantages for dogs that are neutered early in life:

1. Significant reduction in the chance of developing mammary cancer if the ovaries are removed before the female's second, and preferably first, estrous cycle

2. Prevention of ovarian, uterine, testicular, epididymal diseases (such as cancer and infection), and reduction of prostatic problems

3. Prevention of unwanted pregnancies

4. Less surgical and anesthesia time

5. Faster recovery and healing time

6. Fewer behavior problems

7. Elimination of inconveniences associated with a female dog in estrus: vaginal bleeding and discharge that stains furniture and carpets, attracts neighborhood dogs, and leads to accidental mating

In special cases in which surgical neutering is not a safe option, pet owners may explore the possibility of chemical neutering for male dogs. The world's first drug to neuter puppies

All the Wrong "Reasons"

Every veterinarian has heard every wrong "reason," justification, or excuse pet owners have for breeding their dogs. Here are the most common "wrong reasons":

Wrong reason	Truth
Children should experience the "wonder of life" and the birth process by watching their dogs breed, whelp, and raise puppies.	The "wonder" experienced will be at how puppies can eat and defecate so much, be so much hard work, and cost so much to raise. And do not count on the children to participate in any of the work or expense!
Dogs must experience breeding and parenthood to be happy.	Dogs do not need to breed. Raising a litter is hard work that affects the mother's health. Poms often need surgery to deliver pups. Mother Poms can develop mammary or uterine infections, or have problems related to pregnancy and birth. These problems can be difficult and expensive to treat, so your finances can be as seriously affected as your pet's health is threatened.
Breeding will improve the dog's behavior.	Behavior is not improved by breeding, but it may be improved by neutering.
The aging family dog will "have a friend."	A new litter of pups can be very stressful for an aging dog. The older dog may be upset or jealous about the attention the new puppies receive.
The dog's "family line" should be continued.	Very few dogs are so outstanding that the breed needs their genetic contribution. These decisions are best made by knowledgeable Pomeranian breeders who know their dogs' genetics well.
A profit can be made from the sale of the puppies.	This is one of the biggest myths of all! If the mother and pups are properly cared for, receive high-quality nutrition, vaccines, and medications (such as medicine for parasite control), then there will be no profit to be made from the sale of puppies. Good care is expensive and time consuming. Experienced breeders are lucky to break even and usually sell pups at a financial loss, especially if litters are small or surgery (such as C-sections) or medical care are necessary.

was approved by the Food and Drug Administration in March 2003. The drug, chemically known as amino acid 1 arginine and a zinc salt, is injected directly into the testicles and causes atrophy (shrinkage) of the testicles and prostate gland. There are disadvantages to this form of castration:

1. The injection must be administered in the correct place to avoid complications.

2. The animal requires follow-up care and observation to make sure the testicles do not ulcerate.

3. Testosterone (a sex hormone that can cause aggression in some males) secretion is not completely shut off, so the procedure does not help improve behavioral problems associated with aggression.

4. The price of the injection may be similar to the cost of a surgical castration for some animals.

No procedure is completely without risk or side effects. Your veterinarian will advise you about the benefits and possible risks of neutering your Pomeranian and the best technique to use.

By neutering your Pom, you are giving your little friend the best chance for a long, healthy life. You are also doing a humane and community service by not contributing to the pet over-population problem. Every female dog that produces one litter of puppies, has the potential to give rise to 67,000 descendants in a six-year time period. If you think this sounds unbelievable, consider the fact that there are more than 19,000 Pomeranians registered by the American Kennel Club most years in the United States. These animals are the result of planned matings between animals deliberately selected for breeding purposes. Add to that all the other Pomeranians that are not registered, or are produced in puppy mills, and all the unintended breedings that happened "by accident."

It is hard to imagine that any Pomeranian could end up in an animal shelter, rejected, neglected, sick, and unwanted. Sadly, it happens. Pomeranians (and their coats!) need a lot of care and attention. Not everyone is a responsible dog owner. Not everyone will provide, or can afford, the time and expense required to properly care for a Pom.

More than 2,500 dogs are born every hour in the United States. More than 2.1 million dogs are euthanized annually in U.S. animal shelters. That is one dog every fifteen seconds, and Pomeranians number among them. By neutering your Pomeranian, you are helping to reduce these numbers.

Chapter Four

Selecting Your Pomeranian

You know that the Pomeranian is the right *breed* for you, but how do you find just the right *dog*? Selecting your Pom is fun and must be done carefully. After all, you are bringing home a friend that will be part of your family for many years.

The first step in picking a Pom that is the best match for you is to find respected, dedicated Pomeranian breeders. These are the people who know Poms best. You can visit them, see their dogs, and discuss your personal preferences and expectations for a companion. An experienced breeder can help you find a puppy, adolescent, or adult dog to match your desires, personality, and home environment.

Where to Find a Pomeranian

Always buy from a reputable breeder. Finding a good Pomeranian breeder is as important as finding the right Pomeranian. You can find a breeder through the American Pomeranian Club (APC), the American Kennel Club (AKC), or your local dog clubs. These associations can give you a list of respected and dedi-

cated breeders. Attending dog shows and joining a dog club will also give you an opportunity to meet breeders, trainers, and professional dog show handlers who can help put you in contact with the best and most conscientious Pom breeders. If you know someone who has a Pom that you admire, ask who the dog's breeder is. You can also ask your veterinarian for recommendations. Veterinarians see a lot of dogs and know which ones are from healthy backgrounds and which owners take the best care of their animals.

You can also find breeders through advertisements in dog magazines, available from bookstores and pet stores. If you call a breeder from an advertisement, ask for references. And be aware that all responsible breeders will ask *you* for references, such as a veterinary reference or other sources who can confirm that you will give a dog the best of care.

Word of mouth is an excellent way to locate a reputable breeder.

Once you have found some breeders, schedule an appointment to meet them and see their dogs. If you have your heart set on a particular color, ask the breeders what color Poms are available. *Do not rule out a breeder because the color you wanted is not available. Color is not as important as overall health, temperament, and quality.*

Visit as many breeders and kennels as you reasonably can. Compare the quality of their animals and the cleanliness of the facilities. Beware of any breeder who does not want to show you the dogs or the kennels. If a breeder has something to hide, then do not waste your time. Simply move on and visit a different breeder.

Do not be surprised if the breeder you select does not have puppies immediately available. Just remember that a good Pomeranian is well worth the wait. If you are certain you want to be the proud owner of a Pomeranian, it is not too early to start checking with breeders today.

You will know the right puppy when you see it. It will be the healthiest, friendliest, most playful, inquisitive puppy—the one that wants to snuggle with you and seems to say "Take me home!"

Puppy, Adolescent, or Adult?

You may choose to raise a puppy, or prefer to adopt an adolescent or adult dog. Keep an open mind and think about these options carefully. There are advantages and disadvantages to raising a puppy or acquiring an older dog.

Most people want to start with a puppy because they are so cute. A better reason to begin with a pup is so it can be integrated into the family at an early age. A puppy is not a puppy for long. Puppies are temporary beings. In a few short months your puppy will become an adolescent, and a short time after that she will be an adult dog. In the overall life of your dog, four months might be spent with it as a puppy, and more than sixteen years spent with it as an adult. So, do not buy a Pom just because you want a puppy. If you have the opportunity to purchase a wonderful, well-mannered adolescent or adult dog, give it some serious thought. There are some distinct advantages to starting off with a more mature animal that has outgrown some of its naughty behavior attributed to "not knowing any better because she's just a puppy."

Keep the Kids at Home!

Everyone in the family is excited about getting a new Pom puppy—maybe a little bit *too* excited! When you go to visit the breeder and select your Pomeranian, leave the children at home. There are lots of reasons for this excellent, but seemingly austere, advice.

1. Selecting a dog is an adult's decision and responsibility. It requires evaluation and thought. Children fall in love with every pup they see. They want to handle them all and this may not be safe, depending on the age of the children and the puppies. Children can startle and frighten the puppies or their mother, drop or injure a puppy, or be bitten by a protective mother Pom.

2. Children may insist on bringing home a pup that is not the best match for the family. They may resent a new puppy if it is not the one they selected.

3. Children can be distracting. When you are at the breeder's, you need time to discuss important topics, examine pups thoroughly, and concentrate without interruptions, noise, or distractions.

No matter what age Pom you decide to purchase, the most important considerations are health, temperament, and personality. A Pomeranian's personality is well established by the time it is nine to twelve weeks of age. By acquiring a Pom in the very early stages of life, you may influence adult personality and behavioral development in a positive way. This is much easier than trying to change an established undesirable or bad behavior in an adult dog. However, sometimes, for a variety of reasons, a breeder may have an adolescent, young adult, or retired breeder available for sale. If the dog has been well socialized as a youngster and well trained, there are many advantages to purchasing a more mature, older dog. You can skip the trials and tribulations of puppyhood, including housebreaking, leash training, and basic discipline issues such as training your pet not to bark, not to chew on your belongings, and not to rip up your carpet. You must be certain, however, that you and the dog are a good match. It is reasonable to ask for a brief trial period when you purchase an older dog, so that you can be sure the animal will successfully adapt to a new family, environment, and change of lifestyle. A good breeder will encourage this trial period and be willing to take the dog back if she cannot adjust to her new life or if things do not work out as planned within a reasonable time.

Do not be surprised if an older, well-trained Pomeranian is more expensive than a puppy. The adult dog has had a lot more time, effort, and expenses invested in it. No matter what price you pay for your Pom, just keep in mind that it will be insignificant compared with the costs you will incur in feeding, grooming supplies, toys, housing, and veterinary care during the animal's lifetime. So, *save up your money, take your time, and invest in the best.*

Puppies' personalities are well established by nine to twelve weeks of age.

Picking a Pom Puppy

The first rule in selecting a Pomeranian puppy is *know what you want to do with your Pom*. You will be looking for different qualities and traits in your new friend, depending on whether you want to participate in dog shows and competitions, or just want to stay home and enjoy your pet.

The second rule is *take your time*. Do not be an impulse buyer. It is easy to fall in love with the first (and every!) Pom pup you see.

The third rule is to *avoid emotional traps*. Do not buy a pup simply because it is cute or because you feel sorry for it. Do not judge your future companion on looks alone. Looks are important, but health and personality are *extremely* important. If the puppy is not healthy, or if she is shy, continue your search elsewhere. Many

people make the mistake of adopting dogs out of pity because the animals are sick, timid, or runts. Unless you have the emotional fortitude to deal with possible heartbreak later on, and the financial means to pay for extensive and prolonged veterinary care, do not make this mistake. You risk ending up with an animal with serious medical or behavioral problems—and the story could have an unhappy ending if the problems cannot be cured.

Be wise. Take your time, do your homework, and use your head before your heart. It is hard to do, but in the end you will be glad you did. You will have a happy, healthy, outgoing Pom as a companion for many years.

Your Pom pup should not be less than eight weeks old. Some states have laws against selling puppies less than eight weeks of age, and airlines are not allowed to fly puppies younger than eight weeks. At this age a healthy

Good breeders sometimes have a waiting list for their puppies, so start your search now. A quality Pom puppy is well worth the wait.

Pom pup is fully weaned, weighs about 2 pounds (1 kg) or slightly less, and is ready to meet the world.

Once you have located a breeder with Poms for sale, make an appointment to meet the breeder and see the dogs in person. When you find a pup you would like to buy, take time with the breeder to discuss health care, housing, and feeding. Make sure all your questions are answered and ask what type of sales contract the breeder offers—*before* you make the purchase. Verify that the pup is registered with the kennel club. The breeder will sign over the pup's registration papers when you purchase it and provide a copy of the pedigree. Ask the breeder if the puppy or its parents have additional certifications, such as registration by the Canine Eye Registration Foundation (CERF), or any type of testing for freedom from inherited health problems, special examinations (for example, to rule out possible patellar luxation), certifications, or documentation. Ask about any problems that might be in the dog's family lines that are known to occur more frequently in the Pomeranian breed (see "Pomeranian Predispositions: Special Health Concerns").

It is well worth repeating: *The very best way to find a well-socialized, well-bred, healthy Pomeranian puppy is to buy from a reputable breeder.*

Personality

You have selected a Pom puppy with promise and potential. (Let's call him Max.) The first thing to assess is personality. Begin by watching Max in his home environment at the breeder's. Is he happy and outgoing? Is he alert and active, playful and curious? Carefully observe Max and his littermates for signs of good health and happy personalities. A Pomeranian is bright, lively, confident, outgoing, curious, and eager to investigate. After he has had some time to get to know you, Max should be friendly and playful. He might bark at you, and dance forward and backward, but he will be wagging his tail in play as he does. He should not be aggressive or shy.

Physical Condition

Now it is time to check Max's overall physical condition, from his nose to his toes, to make sure he is healthy.

First, check Max's eyes. They should be clear and bright and free of discharge. Max should not be squinting or pawing at his eyes. The membranes inside the eyelids (conjunctiva) should be pink, not bright red and not

Sometimes breeders may offer adolescent or adult Poms for sale. A well-mannered, well-trained, mature Pom can be a wonderful addition to a family.

pale. The ears should be erect, clean, and free of odor, parasites, waxy buildup, or discharge. Gums should be bright pink. Pale or white gums indicate illness, such as anemia, which is often caused by parasitism. Yellowish gums may indicate jaundice or liver problems. If Max is old enough to have lost his baby (deciduous) teeth, make sure they have all completely fallen out where the adult teeth have replaced them. Retained deciduous teeth must be removed, or there will be too many teeth in the mouth. This leads to tooth overcrowding and other dental problems.

Check your Pom puppy carefully. He should be in excellent physical condition, with a beautiful coat, bright-eyed, playful, and alert.

There should never be more than one tooth of the same type in the mouth at one time.

Ideally, Max should have all of his teeth and they should be in correct alignment, although the Pomeranian standard does allow a little leeway and says that one tooth out of alignment in the mouth is acceptable.

Check to be sure that Max's skin and coat are healthy and free of filth, parasites, sores, knots, and mats. Look under the tail to be sure the area is clean and free of signs of blood, diarrhea, tapeworms—or in extreme cases of poor hygiene—maggots (fly larvae).

Feel Max's body. That big furry baby coat can be deceptive. Make sure that the body underneath the coat is not too thin. Max should have a good layer of flesh over the ribs. A full belly from a big meal is one thing, but a grossly distended abdomen with a thin body means there is a health problem, such as intestinal parasites. Feel around the umbilical (navel) area of the abdomen to check for an umbilical hernia. These are common in Poms and are usually of no medical significance. Umbilical hernias can, however, easily be repaired and closed surgically. This is usually done at the same time the dog is neutered.

Conscientious breeders are concerned about placing their puppies in caring, responsible homes. The breeder will ask you questions about

Pomeranian Health Checklist

Attitude	Healthy, alert, playful, inquisitive
Eyes	Bright, clear, free of discharge
Ears	Clean, free of odor, dirt and wax buildup, no evidence of head shaking or scratching
Nose	Clean and free of discharge. The nose may be moist or dry. A cold, damp nose is not unusual. A dry nose does not indicate illness unless it is very hot and crusty with discharge.
Mouth	Gums bright pink, teeth properly aligned, one misaligned tooth is acceptable, no retained deciduous teeth where adult teeth are present
Skin and Coat	Healthy, dense, coat, well groomed, free of knots, tangles, mats, sores, dirt, or parasites
Body Condition	May seem a little plump. A little "baby fat" is all right. A distended belly, a thin body, or visible ribs or hips are signs of health problems, parasites, or poor, inadequate nutrition. Umbilical hernias are common and are not usually a problem, but can be closed surgically.
Movement	Normal gait for a puppy, animated, enthusiastic and a bit bouncy at play

your future plans for Max and the kind of home life you have to offer. This is also your opportunity to ask the breeder questions, so take full advantage of it.

The breeder will surely ask you to take Max to your veterinarian for a complete physical examination within twenty-four to seventy-two hours to confirm his health status and to establish a relationship between you, Max, and your veterinarian. The sooner you take Max in for his examination, the better. If you have any concerns at that time, you can discuss them with your veterinarian and the breeder.

Signs of illness include lack of appetite, depression, inactivity, difficulty breathing, coughing, vomiting, diarrhea, constipation, fever, poor coat quality, and discharge from the ears, nose, eyes or mouth.

Ask to see Max's littermates and parents, if they are present. This will give you a good idea of how you might expect Max to look and behave when he is an adult.

Remember that the way you raise and handle Max, and the people and things he is exposed to as a youngster, will have a big influence on the way his character and temperament develop. Take Max with you on visits and errands and try to introduce him to as many different people and sights and sounds as possible while he is still young and can adapt easily. The time you spend socializing Max as a puppy will help him develop into an outgoing, social, well-adjusted adult.

Important questions to ask the breeder:

1. Which pup would the breeder recommend for you, and why?

2. How old are the pups and what sexes are available?

3. At what age were the pups weaned?

4. How many pups were in the litter?

5. What kind of food is the pup eating at this time? How much? How often?

6. Have the pup and its littermates received any inoculations? If so, which vaccines?

7. Have the pups been wormed or tested for worms?

8. Have the pups had special tests, exams, or certifications? What are the results?

9. How much socialization have the pups received?

10. Has the pup received any basic training (housebreaking, leash training, crate training, car travel)?

11. What type of health guarantee or return policy does the breeder offer?

12. Are the pups registered with the kennel club? If so, is the registration, a full registration or a limited registration?

13. What is the breeder's sale contract?

14. Does the breeder offer a neuter contract?

15. May you see the parents and littermates of the pup?

Male or Female?

Both male and female Pomeranians make wonderful companions. Both will keep you entertained and be faithful friends for life. Pomeranians of either sex are equally affectionate, intelligent, and loyal.

Behavior depends on several factors, including traits inherent in the Pomeranian breed, the animal's own natural individual personality, the type and amount of socialization received as a very young puppy, training throughout life, and the influence of *sex hormones*.

Male Pomeranians can be protective and territorial. Like most male dogs, Poms lift their hind legs to urinate and mark their territory. Male Poms think they rule the house. They are bold and unwilling to back down from anything or anyone. Males can also be a little more challenging to housetrain than females. Neutering

Both males and females make equally wonderful companions. The choice is yours.

(castrating) at an early age can help to reduce some of the testosterone-driven leg lifting, marking, and domineering behaviors, but certainly not the behaviors that are inherited from their Arctic Wolfspitzen ancestors!

Unspayed females present the inconveniences of dealing with estrous cycles every five to eight months. These cycles are under the influence of female sex hormones, particularly progesterone and estrogens. When a female Pom is "in season" or "in heat," she has a bloody vaginal discharge that can stain carpets and furniture and attract unwanted neighborhood male dogs. These problems can be prevented by spaying the female (performing an ovariohysterectomy) at an early age.

Male or female? It's simply a matter of personal preference, and the choice is all yours!

Thinking About Breeding?

If you are thinking of raising and showing Pomeranians in the future, you have to seriously consider your options and discuss these plans with the breeder, who can guide you and help you make the right decisions about which Poms are potentially show dogs and breeding stock.

If you are not planning to breed Pomeranians, you definitely should have your pet, male or female, neutered as early as possible, for reasons previously discussed.

Show Dog or Pretty Pet?

All Pomeranians are wonderful companions, but not all Pomeranians are show dogs. Decide if you want a top-notch show dog for breeding and exhibiting in conformation competitions, or if you want a Pomeranian strictly as a companion and household pet.

The terms *pet quality* and *show prospect* can be confusing. People often interpret *pet quality* to mean the animal has less value or has something wrong with it. The truth is, it is a competitive world out there, and only the very best of the very best have what it takes to win in the show ring. In every dog show there are lots of competitors, but only one walks away with the top award. Many gorgeous dogs never manage to win their titles. So the term *pet quality* is not intended to mean something is wrong with a Pom, but simply that it may not match all aspects of the Pomeranian breed standard required to win that elusive championship title. The differences between a "show dog" and a "strictly

Most novice breeders begin by investing in the best female they can find, often an adult that has proven herself in the show ring and/or previously produced a high-quality litter. Then, with the help of an experienced breeder, the novice finds the most suitable stud dog for the female and pays for its services. In between time, the novice also learns as much as possible about the breed and participates in dog show activities, often under the mentorship of the breeder.

One of the things breeders dread most is selling a puppy as a "pet," only to learn later that the dog was used for breeding or exhibiting. Not all Poms meet the rigorous standard of perfection for a show dog, and not all Poms should be used for breeding. So be sure to share your plans for your Pom with the breeder before you buy.

Ask the breeder to see your puppy's parents. This will give you an idea of what your puppy might look like when he is an adult.

companion dog" are not readily apparent to many people. The nuances that set your Pom apart from a show Pom may be slight and detected only by the trained eye of an experienced breeder or show judge.

A "pet-quality" Pom may have minor imperfections with regard to the tough requirements needed to be a "show" Pom and become a champion, but that does not stop your dog from being extraordinary in all other respects. If your Pom is absent from the conformation ring, that means more time for the obedience and agility rings, more time for pet-facilitated therapy work and community service, more time for family and friends, and more time for walks in the park with you! There are many different ways to show off your Pom. Being a pet-quality Pom is just another way of winning.

If you have decided that you definitely want a show dog, be prepared to pay a lot more for it than you would pay for a pet quality Pom. In fact, many show Poms sell for more than three times the amount of a pet Pom. Also, keep in mind that although the parents may be champion show dogs, there is no guarantee that your show-prospect Pom puppy will turn out to be a champion, too. After all, it is a "prospect." The assumption that your Pom will turn out to be a competitive show dog is based on its relatives, its pedigree, and what it looks like today. Even the most promising Pom pup can change as it grows up and may not reach the full show potential you had hoped. If you buy a puppy, you are betting, or hoping, that it will attain a certain level of conformational quality after it has completed all its development and growth phases. A lot of changes can take place between puppyhood and adulthood.

If you are serious about purchasing a show dog, consider buying an adult Pomeranian that has already proven successful in the show ring. When you buy an adult, what you see is what you get and there is no guesswork involved. If you are fortunate enough to obtain a show-quality animal from a breeder, show it and campaign it!

Pedigree and Registrations

Before making a final decision and completing the sale, be sure Max's health records, pedigree, and registration papers are in order. A puppy should have a health certificate signed by a veterinarian saying the puppy has been examined and is in good health and able to travel. Dates of inoculations and any medications (such as worming or other anti-parasite medications) should be noted on the health certificate. Your veterinarian will need this information to set up a preventive health care program for Max.

One of the many pleasures of owning a purebred Pomeranian is pride of ownership and the variety of activities in which you and your canine companion can participate. For example, without registration papers, there is no proof of parentage or lineage. When you purchase Max, be sure to verify that both of his parents are registered and that he has been registered as well. Do not confuse official registration with a pedigree. A pedigree is not an official document. It is a chart showing the names of your dog's family members. In other words, it is his genealogy, naming parents, grandparents, and great-grandparents. The pedigree may include three or more generations. A pedigree does not guarantee that your dog is registered with the kennel club. Registration is an official document issued by the kennel club and is proof that your dog is purebred. However, if Max is registered with the American Kennel Club, you can purchase his official pedigree, suitable for framing, directly from the AKC.

You should receive application papers from the breeder to register Max, showing you as the new owner. Once you choose a name, complete the application form and mail it to the kennel club address on the application with the appropriate registration fee. The name you use to register your Pom may be different than his call name, or nickname. For example, you might call your Pom Max, but you might give him a fancy, longer name for his official registration. The breeder might request that you use the breeder's kennel name as a prefix to Max's registered name, so that Pom aficionados will know his kennel of origin and his breeder.

If you purchase Max as a young puppy born in the United States, the breeder will give you one of the following AKC forms:

1. Dog Registration Application

This is an 8½ by 11 inch (21 by 27.5 cm) document that indicates the name and address of the breeder, the dog's litter registration number, its birth date, and the names and registration numbers of the dog's parents. There are spaces to write in the dog's new registered name, its color, and its sex. The new owner's name, address, telephone number, and e-mail address also must be included. The breeder indicates on the document whether the dog is to receive a full registration or a limited registration. The person registering the animal has the right to name it. After the registration application is completed, it must be signed by both the breeder and the new owner, and co-owners, if any. The new owner then sends the document to the AKC with the appropriate fee, indicated on the application form. At this time the new owner can also purchase a certified pedigree of the dog directly from the AKC.

2. Full Registration

Full registration comes as a white slip of paper with a purple border. It indicates the dog's registered name and AKC number, the dog's birth date, breed, sex, and color, the breeder, and the owner. Full registration allows for participation in AKC competitions and events, as well as

A special puppy deserves a special name. The official registered name can be long and fancy, but keep the call name short and simple.

the ability to register future offspring of the animal with the AKC.

3. Limited Registration

The limited registration form looks exactly like a full registration certificate, except the border is orange. It provides the same documentation as full registration. Dogs with limited registration are not to be used for breeding or exhibition in conformation shows. If they are bred, their puppies cannot be registered with the AKC. Dogs with limited registration are welcome to participate in many other AKC events, such as agility and obedience competitions.

The breeder is the only person who can change an animal's status from limited to full registration.

Chapter Five

At Home with Your Pomeranian

Your perfect Pom puppy charmed her way right into your heart. It is time to welcome this soft little ball of fluff into your home, knowing that from now on, your life will never be the same. Life will be more fun with the affection, joy, and entertainment your little companion will give you for the next several years. All you have to do is keep her safe and take good care of her—and love her in return.

Pom Preparations

Be ready for your new arrival *before* you bring her home. Start by making sure your house and yard are safe, because once you set this tiny baby on the ground, she will transform into a busybody adventurer, eager to explore every inch of your house and yard. She will not miss a thing. Where there is danger lurking, she will find it. And being inquisitive— as all Poms are—she could get into big trouble.

Make sure your house and yard are safe before you bring your puppy home!

Have everything ready in advance that your little newcomer will need. This makes it easier for Charm to adapt to her new life and home with you. If your Pom feels comfortable and secure, the transition period will go smoothly for both of you.

Travel Crate

One of the first, best, and most important purchases you will make is a travel crate, also called a flight kennel. A travel crate is a must! Part of what makes Poms so much fun is their portable size. With a travel crate you can take your Pom almost everywhere you go—starting with her first trip home.

Most Pomeranian breeders use travel crates to prepare their puppies from a very early age for leaving home, travel training, and housebreaking. Pom pups retain their ancient ancestors' instinct to use a den for security and sleeping. A travel crate serves that purpose perfectly. Poms love to play, store their toys, and sleep inside crates. Poms are also very clean and would never intentionally soil their den area. They will not urinate or defecate in their crates unless they have been closed inside them much too long. When Charm is old

An exercise pen lets you safely confine your Pom when necessary and provides enough space for your Pom to play.

enough, you can take advantage of this fact by using a crate for some of her housetraining lessons (see "Housetraining Your Pomeranian").

A travel crate should always be a pleasant place for your Pom. Never confine her to a crate for long periods of time or it will seem more like a prison to her than a den.

Ideally, the breeder will have already introduced Charm to a travel kennel. If possible, give the breeder a soft blanket for Charm a day or two before bringing her home. You can then place the blanket in the travel kennel for the trip home. A familiar item with familiar scents will make her feel more secure during the trip home and for the next few days in her new environment.

It is not unusual for puppies to be carsick or soil their crates the first few times they travel. Allow Charm to relieve herself before you place her in the travel crate. If the trip home is short, you can reduce chances of carsickness by withholding food two hours before travel so your Pom will be less likely to feel nauseated or vomit. However, if the trip home is a long one, you will need to stop often to let her eliminate. Young Pom puppies must have food available at all times and must have plenty of water so they do not become dehydrated.

For travel comfort, place Charm's blanket on top of some towels or a layer of newspapers. If Charm feels queasy, she may drool excessively, so bring along plenty of paper towels and a plastic bag, just in case.

Do not let your Pom out to urinate or defecate at public parks or rest stops. She can be exposed to serious diseases in these locations. Instead, place her in a clean area and allow her to do her business on newspapers or pads.

Travel Safety

Because Charm will be your constant traveling companion, travel safety is the first thing she must learn. Rule

Supplies for Your New Pomeranian

1. Travel kennel: for travel, training, safety, privacy, and sleeping area. Ideal for use as a den or small doghouse. Crates are lightweight, easy to clean, and well ventilated.
2. Food and water dishes or water bottles with sipper tubes. Use solid, no-spill, stainless steel dishes or ceramic crocks. Do not use plastic dishes.
3. High-quality puppy/dog food
4. Comfortable bedding or big pillow: bedding should be made of natural materials (cotton, wool). Synthetic materials or bedding containing cedar shavings can cause allergies.
5. First aid kit
6. Collar or harness (breakaway cat collar for baby Pom)
7. Leash (slender and lightweight show lead)
8. Identification tag
9. Grooming supplies: small slicker brush, soft-bristle brush, wide-toothed metal comb, blunt-tipped scissors, nail trimmers (guillotine-style), styptic powder, gentle emollient shampoo, ear-cleaning solution, cotton balls
10. Dental supplies: soft toothbrush, dog toothpaste
11. Exercise pen (X-pen): portable, folding pen, available in a variety of sizes, with attachments for dishes and water bottles
12. Safety gate: needed for closing off areas or stairways to prevent escape or injury. Do not use accordion-folding styles. These can fold in and close tightly on your Pom's feet, legs, body, or neck, causing serious injuries, breaks, or suffocation.
13. Other type of safe, escape-proof, large enclosure, such as a cage crate with a solid pan floor.
14. Toys: soft stuffed toys, ball. Remove small parts that could be swallowed or cause choking, such as buttons, bells, whistles.
15. Housebreaking pads: available from the pet stores, also called "wee pads"
16. Pooper scooper

number one: Poms must stay in travel crates whenever they are in the car!

Your new companion may protest all the way home, or, if she is already used to a travel crate, will probably sleep. If Charm cries, talk to her soothingly so she knows she is not alone. Make the firm decision right now not to give in to her whimpering, no matter how difficult it is to ignore her. Do not hold her in the car. If you do, she will not forget it, and she will expect you to hold her on your lap every car trip you take together.

No dog should ever be loose in a car, especially a small Pomeranian. In the event of an accident, your Pom could be injured by an airbag, thrown into a window, or flung from the vehicle. She could also cause an accident

by getting underfoot by the gas and brake pedals, being caught in the steering wheel, or distracting the driver. It is safer for everyone on the road if Charm remains in her travel kennel whenever she is in the car. So be firm in your resolve when it comes to travel safety.

Welcome Home!

When you arrive home, give your Pomeranian a small drink of water and allow her to relieve herself. House-training starts from this moment on, so choose a spot where you want Charm to do her eliminations in the future. She may not do her toilet duties right away, so be patient and give her a little time to explore the area.

Your Pom will be very tired from her trip and all the excitement. She will need some quiet time to herself. Puppies tire quickly. If Charm is sleepy, allow her to rest. If she feels like becoming acquainted, make introductions calmly and gently. Avoid loud noises and sudden movements. Teach children in the home to respect her space and privacy.

Your Pom will feel more comfortable and be happier if you keep a daily routine or schedule. Dogs are creatures of habit and enjoy regular mealtimes, walks, games, and naps. Do not expect everything to go per-

fectly the first few days your new companion is home with you. Whether you bring home a puppy or an adult dog, there will be a period of adjustment before your pet feels completely at ease.

The "settling in" period is very important. It sets the tone for the future relationship you and your Pomeranian will establish. The lifelong bond that you will enjoy with Charm begins the

Check fencing carefully to be sure your Pom cannot escape from your yard.

day she comes home. As you teach your new friend about good manners, mealtimes, traveling, and sleeping arrangements remember: *Patience, kindness, and consistency are the keys to successfully raising and training a Pomeranian.*

Handle with Care!

Teach children in the home the correct way to lift and handle a small Pomeranian, by gently putting one hand under the chest and the other

Poms should be housed indoors and be allowed to go outside often to play.

under the hindquarters for support. Never lift a Pomeranian by the scruff of the neck or by the limbs. Very small children should not lift or handle Pomeranians, especially puppies, as they can drop or injure them. Older children should remain seated on the floor when petting or handling a Pom. It is very important that children learn from the beginning that Pomeranians are tiny, delicate, sensitive beings and not toys.

Naming Your Pomeranian

Your Pomeranian has her own unique personality. As you get to know her better, you will think of a name that suits your little friend and fits her character perfectly. If you need some ideas, there are plenty of names in dog books, magazines, and baby books.

It seems easier for most dogs to recognize names with one or two syllables. Some dog trainers recommend two syllable names to avoid confusion with one syllable commands such as *come, sit, stay*, and *down*. However, Poms are smarter than many dogs, and one-syllable names are not a problem for them.

As soon as you have chosen a name for your Pom, use it often when speaking to her. It won't take long for her to recognize her name and know who she is. In fact, don't be surprised later on when, as your Pom learns more of your words and mannerisms, she even knows when you are talking *about* her to someone!

Once your Pom knows her name, you can usually get her attention when you want it. When she responds or comes to you, praise her lavishly. Congratulations! You have just started verbal communication—the first step in your pet's lifelong training!

Housing Considerations

Your Pom may have a plush coat, but she is definitely an indoor pet for many reasons. First and foremost, she wants to be the center of family attention and be included in family activities. Charm may act like a big tough dog because her ancestral instincts tell her that is what she is. But realistically, if you live in the country, she is no match for raccoons, coyotes, and large stray dogs. A tiny Pom puppy can also easily fall prey to wild predator birds, such as hawks.

Charm is an indoor dog also because she is tiny. Even with her thick double coat, her surface area to body mass ratio is such that she will lose body heat if left outside in very cold weather. She can also overheat in hot weather and suffer from heatstroke. Keep Charm safe. Let her play in the yard, but make sure she has shelter and water at all times. Never leave your Pom outside unsupervised. Let her live indoors and share the comforts of home with you.

When you bring Charm home, choose a safe place where you can set up an X-pen (exercise pen) and place her travel crate inside the pen.

You should protect your Pom puppy from household dangers by keeping her in an enclosed pen. Make sure the pen is close enough to family activities so your Pom won't feel isolated.

Make sure the location is near family activities, such as near the kitchen or living room, so she does not feel lonely or isolated. Charm should feel secure and have her privacy, yet be able to watch the activities and be observed. Exposure to different people, sights, sounds, smells, and activities are very important aspects of puppy socialization.

Place your Pom in the area to explore and relax for several minutes. Feed her a little treat and praise her. Charm should associate her space with enjoyment. Your pet does not know the rules yet and she will need training, so make sure her den is in an area where she cannot chew furniture, baseboards, or electrical cords; soil the carpet; or get into trouble. Later, when you have started training Charm, do not use her pen and crate areas as places to go when she is punished. Her territory should always be a comforting place where she goes when all is right with the world, and not when she is in trouble.

If you have acquired an older Pomeranian, try to duplicate her previous housing situation as much as possible to reduce the stress of changing her home environment.

Pom-Proofing Your Home

Imagine you are very tiny and curious. Now examine your home and yard—at Pomeranian eye level and at Pomeranian jumping height. Keep in mind the fact that Poms are excellent jumpers. What things do you see that Charm could investigate, crawl under, pull down, get trapped in, get caught between, jump up on, fall off of, run

Poms are clever and curious. They can push doors and open cabinets. Many household products are poisonous for Poms. If you think your Pom has come in contact with a dangerous product, take her to your veterinarian immediately, even if you are not sure.

into, chew on, or eat? Suddenly your cozy home looks like a jungle. The list of potential dangers to your dog is a long one.

Pomeranians are small, active, and bold. These appealing traits also make them more accident prone. There are many potentially life-threatening situations in your home—accidents just waiting to happen. Before you bring Charm home and allow her to explore, you must remove any possible hazards.

Household Cleaning Products and Chemicals

Cleaning products and chemicals are potentially deadly for Charm if she comes in contact with them. Make sure cabinets are closed and securely latched.

Pom puppies love to chew! Wooden baseboards and walls are easy to gnaw on and their paints can be toxic, especially in older buildings with lead-based paints.

Toilet-cleaning chemicals and toilet fresheners are also toxic. You might think Charm is not tall enough to reach the water in the toilet, but Poms are clever, curious, and determined. They can scramble and climb into the most unlikely places. If Charm drinks from the toilet, the chemicals can harm her. Worse yet, she might fall inside the toilet bowl. As strange as it sounds, this is a common accident. Pups that fall inside the toilet bowl often cannot climb out. Charm could become very cold or even drown. *Keep the seat down on the toilet!*

Antifreeze

Antifreeze (ethylene glycol) is a common cause of animal poisoning. Animals are attracted to this sweet-tasting automotive chemical that can be found on garage floors. Sadly, drinking even a very small amount causes severe kidney damage and often death. Survival depends on an early diagnosis and immediate treatment. Do not allow Charm in the garage where she might lick a few drops of antifreeze off of the floor.

There is a type of antifreeze available that is said to be nontoxic to animals. This product may be available in your area.

Make sure gates are closed and securely latched, to prevent accidental loss and injury.

Rodent Poisons and Snap Traps

Rodent bait is as deadly for Charm as it is for wild vermin. Even if you do not use mouse, rat, or gopher bait, your neighbor might. Rodents can roam the neighborhood before the poison takes full effect and kills them, so check your yard and garage for dead rodents. Pomeranians are curious and will investigate and play with anything they find. If Charm eats part of a poisoned animal, she can be poisoned as well.

If you have snap traps set in your house or garage, remove them. They can easily break your Pom's delicate toes or injure her nose.

Electrical Shock

Make sure Charm does not chew on electrical cords or wiring. She could die from electrocution or suffer from electrical burns. She could also cause an electrical fire in your home.

Kitchen and Appliances

Poms are constantly underfoot, making the kitchen a dangerous place. You could trip over your Pom or she could be burned by hot liquids spilling over from a pot on the stove.

Laundry areas are also hazardous. Before you load the laundry into the washer, make sure Charm is not napping in the clothes pile. Check the dryer, too. Incredibly, many small pets have been found, too late, inside the dryer.

Doors, Windows, and Furniture

Make sure all doors to the outside or to the garage are securely closed. Pomeranians love to jump up on furni-

Poms love to jump on the furniture, but they can also fall off. Many Pomeranian bone fractures are caused from falling off of furniture.

ture and look out the window. Windows and screens should be securely fastened so that Charm cannot fall out the window. Many Pomeranian bone fractures are caused from falling, not just out of windows but off of furniture as well.

If you have sliding glass windows, place decals on them at Charm's eye level. Many Pomeranian injuries are caused by running into sliding glass doors.

Close doors carefully. Charm can be seriously injured if she is caught in a closing door. If she slips through the door to the great outdoors undetected, she can become lost or may die from an automobile accident, wild animals, or harsh weather.

Injuries from Humans and Animals

Get ready to learn the Pom shuffle! Pomeranians are small, always close by, and move quickly. Their bones are delicate and break easily. Charm can be underfoot before you know it and be stepped on and hurt. You will find yourself shuffling your feet for the first few weeks, just trying not to step on your Pom, or trying to sidestep her, keep your balance, and not trip or fall over her.

Most Pomeranian cases of broken bones or injuries are caused by owners accidentally stepping on them, children dropping them, or larger dogs attacking them or playing too roughly with them.

Poisonous Plants and Yard Chemicals

Many ornamental and garden plants are toxic to animals, including philodendron, dieffenbachia, foxglove, and lilies. Keep household plants out of reach and limit home and garden plants to nontoxic varieties. If you think a plant is toxic, check with the nursery or grower before you purchase it.

Many yard chemicals and fertilizers are poisonous to pets. Be sure to check labels.

Foreign Objects

Pomeranians explore with their mouths, especially puppies. They will eat the most unusual things, even if they do not taste good. And because Poms have such small throats, even the smallest item can cause choking or obstruct the throat and airways.

Make sure small balls, children's toys, rubber bands, paper clips, pens, sewing needles, pins, and any other objects are out of your pet's reach. Coins are a special hazard because pennies contain high levels of zinc, which is very toxic. Be sure that any toys you purchase are safe and do not contain small pieces, buttons, bells, or whistles that may present a choking hazard.

Garbage

As unappealing as it is to us, garbage is attractive to dogs. As a result, they often suffer from "garbage poisoning," a form of poisoning caused by bacteria and toxins found in old and decaying foods. Poms may also suffer

Many ornamental plants are toxic. Check your garden to be sure it is safe for your Pom.

from eating dangerous items in the garbage, such as bones, aluminum foil, and plastic wrap. The list of hazards in the trash can is endless.

Candies and Medicines

Make sure you have not left any foods or medicine containers within Charm's reach. An overdose of common medicines, including aspirin, acetaminophen (Tylenol), ibuprofen (Advil, Motrin), and naproxen (Aleve), can be fatal for her. Chocolate contains caffeine and theobromine, two methylxanthine substances toxic to dogs. Hard candies can get stuck in the teeth, jaw, or throat and cause choking or suffocation. Some artificial sweeteners in candies are toxic to dogs.

Holidays are a time when dogs run into trouble because owners leave

Identification

If Charm is ever lost, your chances of being reunited are very slim without proper identification. Ninety percent of all lost family pets do not have identification. Seventy percent of these animals never return home. Every year, millions of lost pets are euthanized in the United States. Do not let your Pom become one of the statistics.

Identification is easy. It is also inexpensive, especially when compared with the costs of dealing with losing a pet: hours of searching, sleepless nights worrying; time making "lost pet" posters; long-distance telephone calls; the cost of placing advertisements in newspapers; and checking the animal shelters. And after all that effort, you may not even have the good fortune to pay someone the reward money for finding your pet. Too many lost dogs' stories have sad endings.

If Charm does not yet have identification, stop whatever you are doing and *have her identified right now*. You will be glad you did.

Microchips

One of the best forms of permanent animal identification is a microchip. A microchip is a tiny transponder about the size of a grain of rice that is implanted under the skin quickly and easily by injection. Many Pomeranian breeders have their puppies microchipped before they sell

sweets out on the coffee table for all the family to share. Your little Pom can smell the goodies and stand up to reach the table—and she will help herself to as much as she wants!

Swimming Pools

If you own a pool, make sure your Pom cannot access it. If she falls into the pool, she will not be able to pull herself out, and without assistance she will drown. If possible, put a fence around the pool or cover it.

Make a special ramp for your Pom to climb out of the pool, in case she accidentally falls in, and train her how to use it. An escape ramp and training can save her life.

Paper Shredders

Turn your paper shredder off when you are not using it. There have been several cases of curious dogs losing their tongues from licking paper shredders that were set on "automatic feed."

Microchips for Overseas Travelers

The United States and foreign countries use different microchips and scanners. Some U.S. microchips cannot be detected by scanners used in foreign countries. Many countries require that your pet be microchipped before you bring it in. If you are traveling overseas with your Pomeranian, ask your veterinarian to obtain a microchip that can be read in foreign countries and to place it in the correct area as required by the country you will be visiting.

Ask your veterinarian to microchip your Pom. This will increase the chances of finding your Pom in case of loss or theft.

them. If Charm has already been identified this way, her breeder will give you the information and necessary papers to let the registry know you are the new owner.

If Charm is not yet microchipped, your veterinarian can do the job in a few seconds. In the United States the microchip is placed between the shoulder blades at the base of the neck. In some countries the microchip is placed on the left shoulder.

Each microchip has a unique series of numbers so that each animal has its own identification number. A handheld scanner, also called a decoder or reader, reads the identification number. Scanning is painless and accurate. Microchips are safe, permanent, and tamper-proof.

Once an animal has been implanted with a microchip, the following information is entered into a central computer registry: animal's identification number, a description of the animal, the owner's name, address, and telephone number, and an alternate contact in case the owner cannot be reached. It is the owner's responsibility to update the registry in the event of a change in information. An identification tag for the animal's collar also is provided, indicating the animal's identification number and the registry's telephone number.

Lost animals can be identified at animal shelters, humane societies, and veterinary offices. Once the animal's identification number is displayed, the central registry is contacted and the owner is contacted.

Surprisingly, the cost for all of this technology, including the microchip and its implantation, is modest. At the time of this writing, it is approximately $40. In addition, the price for lifetime

Prevent Choking and Strangulation!

Slip martingale or choke collars are dangerous for Pomeranians unless they have been trained to these types of collars.

Never leave your Pomeranian unattended wearing a slip or choke collar. The collar can accidentally catch or hang on objects and your pet could strangle to death.

Never tie your Pomeranian to an object, no matter what type of collar she is wearing.

enrollment in the American Kennel Club Animal Recovery database is currently only $12.50. For the life of your pet, this is one of the best investments you can make.

Collars, Harnesses, and Name Tags

A name tag is an excellent form of identification that can be attached to a collar or harness. A cat collar is a nice option for a tiny Pom because it will not slip over the head as easily as a buckle collar, is small and gentle on the neck, and does not damage the coat.

Make sure the collar fits correctly. You should be able to fit two fingers between the collar and your Pom's neck. Check the collar daily to be sure it is not too tight as your pet (and her hair!) grow.

A comfortable, nonslip harness is a good alternative for Poms, especially youngsters who have not yet fine-tuned their leash-walking skills. Again, check the harness frequently to be sure your Pom has not outgrown it. Also, as Charm grows a fuller coat, the harness could become too tight.

Many pet stores offer name-tag engraving. Collars, harnesses, and tags are easy to see and let others know your lost friend has a family.

Tattoos

Tattoos are a good form of identification because they are a permanent and visible way of saying an animal has an owner. However, they are not a good identification alternative for Pomeranians because it is difficult to tattoo several numbers on their small

A light lead and a break-away cat collar are good training options for a Pom puppy. To prevent strangulation, never leave a collar or lead on your puppy when it is left alone and never tie your puppy to any objects.

Identify Your Pomeranian Today!

The best thing you can do to increase the chances for a safe return of your lost, injured, or stolen pet is give her as many forms of identification as possible.

1. All dogs should have a collar or harness and an identification tag.

2. All dogs should be micro-chipped and registered with the microchip registry.

3. All dogs should be registered with the American Kennel Club Animal Recovery Database.

4. Consider having your Pomeranian tattooed.

inner thigh or belly. Also, tattoos are difficult to see because of the thick coat.

Most veterinarians offer tattoo identification for dogs. If you decide to have Charm tattooed, do not rely entirely on this method to help you be reunited if she is ever lost. There are several tattoo registries. They recommend using numbers that will not change, such as your dog's AKC number or your Social Security number. These are long numbers, and finding room to write them on a small Pomeranian is a big challenge. If you wish to tattoo your Pom, it is better to use her AKC number and register her with the AKC Companion Animal Recovery Database. The Internal Revenue Service can find you when it wants tax money, but it is not a dog registry and will not assist in finding you to reunite you with your pet.

One good thing about tattoos is that most animal shelters will give a tattooed animal a grace period of a few additional days before euthanizing it. You can also prove the dog belongs to you, in case of theft. Tattoos are helpful, but should never be used as a sole source of animal identification.

Housetraining Your Pomeranian

Pomeranians are clean, smart, and easy to housetrain. With encouragement, praise, and the right kind of training, it will not take long for your Pom to learn the rules of toilet etiquette. Poms learn even faster if there are other dogs in the home that are already housetrained. The keys to successful housetraining are patience, diligence, consistency, frequent toilet breaks, making sure your Pom gets to the right place at the right time, and—of course—lots of praise.

Pomeranians are meticulous about their living quarters and do their best not to soil them. This is another good reason for keeping Charm in a travel kennel on the way home from the breeder's. If the trip is not too long, she will probably wait to urinate or defecate. You can start out right by taking her outside immediately upon arrival and placing her right where you want her to learn to do her business. Give her plenty of time. When she does eliminate, praise her. You are off to a positive start!

Next, place Charm in her designated living area. This area should have easy-to-clean, nonslip flooring, and should not be carpeted. Remember that Charm has a very small bladder and does not have full control of her bladder or bowels yet. She will need to go outside frequently and certainly will have a few accidents before she is fully trained. When a puppy has an accident in the house, it is not the puppy's fault. Either she has not yet learned where she is supposed to go, or she was not taken out soon enough or often enough. It is up to *you* to prevent accidents in the house by taking your Pom out frequently and recognizing signs when she needs to eliminate.

Poms want to please. As soon as your puppy understands that she should urinate or defecate only in the specific area you have indicated, she will try her best to wait until you take her to that spot. If she soils in her confinement, it is an accident, so do not punish her. *Never* resort to cruel, unsuccessful, disciplinary measures of long ago, such as rubbing a dog's nose in its urine, or hitting it. These are the worst things you can do.

Scolding

If your Pom has an accident, do not raise your voice. If you scold your puppy, she may become confused and behave just the opposite of how you would like. She may become less sociable, fearful, or withdraw from you. Or, she may become resentful. She will not associate your scolding with her natural body functions, especially if the scolding occurs some time after the act of elimination.

Be reasonable. Everything is new and strange to your baby Pom, and like all babies, she has little control over her elimination at this point. Rather, clean up the mess and work on positive reinforcement by praising her profusely when she does the right thing.

Watch for Signs

Charm does not yet know how to tell you when she needs to go outside. For now, it is up to you to be attentive to her needs and signs of impending urination or defecation so you can take her outside in time. Signs include sniffing the ground, pacing, circling, whining, crying, and acting anxious. You must act fast as soon as this behavior begins or you will be too late! Charm will always need to eliminate *immediately* after waking up from a nap or after eating a

Very Bad Advice!

You may have heard that if a puppy soils in its crate, it should be confined in the crate for thirty minutes along with its excrements. This cruel and unsuccessful training method is based on the idea that a puppy will be so miserable it will try harder to hold itself next time. The truth is, your Pom would not be the only miserable individual. You will be, too! You will have an even bigger mess to clean up because your puppy will be forced to step or lie in her feces. She will get everything everywhere, including in her hair. You will then have the crate *and* your puppy to clean.

meal, so in these instances, take her directly outside without waiting for signs. Remember to lavish praise on her for her performance.

Schedules

One of the keys to successful housetraining is to set up a regular schedule to let Charm out to do her business. A good schedule for housetraining is to take your puppy out to the potty area every two hours. Be patient and wait until she goes, then praise her and play with her. If your puppy wants to stay and play in the yard, let her play for a while before bringing her back into the house. If you always make your Pom go back indoors immediately after eliminating, she might refuse to eliminate because she will associate those actions with the end of playtime in the yard.

If your Pom does not relieve herself, bring her back inside and put her directly in her travel crate for thirty minutes. Do not leave her in the crate more than thirty minutes. Then take her directly outside again. After Charm eliminates, praise her and play with her for a few minutes in the yard

How Often Is Often Enough?

Puppies should be let outside, or placed on newspaper in a designated area, to urinate every two to three hours. If your puppy has just eaten, there is more pressure on the urinary bladder, and it should be placed in its toilet area immediately to prevent an accident.

Housetraining Tips

1. Start housetraining your Pomeranian the day she arrives—it is never too early.
2. Make sure your puppy is receiving good nutrition, has normal stools, and is free of internal parasites.
3. Keep your Pomeranian on a regular feeding schedule and do not feed her table scraps or excess treats during the training period.
4. Let your puppy outside several times a day, first thing in the morning, after every meal, after naps, and as late as possible in the evening.
5. Never scold your puppy if she has an accident.
6. Praise your Pom profusely when she does the right thing.
7. Learn to recognize the signs when your puppy needs to go outside.
8. Be patient and understanding. Never scold and never spank.

and then take her to the house to play (supervised, of course!). She will not take long at all to realize that when she goes outside, she is supposed to do her business and is rewarded with praise and playtime.

Most of your puppy's time will be spent with you, or in a safe, confined area. *When you have to be out of the house for long periods of time and cannot take your pet outside, do not crate her.* Keep her in a restricted, enclosed area and cover the floor with newspa-

Crate Training Guidelines

Total maximum crate time for a Pom pup daily	Age
Two hours	8 to 12 weeks
Three hours	12 to 16 weeks
Four hours	16 to 20 weeks
Overnight, no more than six hours	20 weeks and older

pers. Charm will do her best to urinate and defecate on the papers. She has the right idea and is learning to control her elimination until she reaches a given spot, even if it is on a newspaper and not always in the backyard.

Leave your pet's crate in the confined area and take the door off so she can use the crate as a den. When you need to confine Charm to her crate, it just takes a moment to replace the door.

Crate Training

The kennel crate is an ideal house-training tool. If you crate Charm for part of the night, give her plenty of bedding and line the crate with absorbent material. Charm will do her best not to soil her sleeping quarters. Just be sure to get up early to let her outside. It is unfair for you to sleep in and make a puppy wait for a long time with a very full bladder!

When you take Charm out to potty, be patient and stay and wait with her. She should not be left alone. If you go into the house, she may become worried and try to find you, or become distracted and forget why she has been let outside. And if you are in the house, you will not know for sure if Charm did anything. You may bring her inside

before she has finished and she could have an accident in the house shortly afterward. That is a preventable setback in the training program.

In Case of an Accident on the Carpet

There are several carpet-cleaning products designed specifically for removal of pet odors and stains. Some of these are available from your veterinarian or your local supermarket. However, if you do not have any of these commercial products immediately available, and if your puppy accidentally soils the carpet, here are two simple solutions that may help. You may try one or the other, but be sure to test a small section of your carpet first, to be sure the solution does not damage it.

1. Mix one part clear (white) vinegar to one part water and lightly dab or blot on carpet with a clean towel.
2. Take a small amount of club soda and dab it lightly on the carpet and blot it dry with a clean towel.

The Courteous Cleanup Crew—*You!*

• When you take your pet outside, do not forget the essentials! Take a plastic bag or a "pooper scooper" to promptly pick up the mess and discard it properly in a well-sealed plastic bag. Do not bury the excrements in the ground where it can be stepped on or other animals can find it.

• Dog feces may contain contagious organisms that can spread diseases such as parvovirus or intestinal parasites. Some of these are contagious to other dogs and some are contagious to people.

• Be courteous. Keep your environment pristine and safe for everyone to enjoy.

Let Me Out!

You can teach your Pom how to ask to go outside by using a safe squeaker toy or a little bell on a cord. Fasten the toy or bell to your door, within your pet's reach. Every time you take her outside, squeak the toy, or ring the bell, immediately before leaving the house. Poms are smart, and your Pom will quickly associate the squeak or ring with going outside and eliminating. Do not be surprised when your Pom starts squeaking the toy or ringing the bell when she needs to go outside. And do not be surprised if she cleverly takes advantage of her new trick to also ask to go outside just to play!

When Charm is a little older, you can restrict her to her crate for brief periods of time when you have to be away. When you return, be sure to take Charm outside immediately.

Do not use the crate for housetraining if you have to be away for extended periods of time.

Check for Problems

Be sure that your Pom eliminates normally. If she is constipated, or has diarrhea or worms, you may not notice unless you are in the yard and see what she does. (In those cases, collect a fresh stool sample to take to your veterinarian for diagnosis.) If your Pom is having difficulty urinating or has blood in her urine, she may have a bladder or kidney infection or stones and should see your veterinarian immediately.

Pomeranians will not intentionally soil their houses, dens, or sleeping areas. If your pet has an accident, it is because she had to wait longer than she was capable. The best way to prevent toilet accidents is to take your puppy outside more often.

Housetraining is the result of two-way communication. You teach Charm that she must eliminate outside, and she must find a way to let you know her desire to go outside when nature calls. She may never ask to go outside by barking or scratching at the door or fetching her leash like the dogs in the movies. But if she has not been outside for a long period of time, or just woke up, or finished a meal, or acts anxious or apprehensive and starts to pant and stare at you, you know what to do.

Poms love to run and play. Exercise on flat, soft surfaces, such as sand or grass, softens the impact on bones and is good for Poms of any age, including pups with growing bones and older Poms with arthritis.

Exercise and Games

Pomeranians are very active dogs that love to go on walks and play games. Regular daily exercise is important for your Pom's health. If she does not get enough exercise, she may become overweight, bored, or depressed, or find something mischievous and destructive to do to keep her busy.

Your Pomeranian does not need a large backyard to keep in shape—she needs *you*! Your pet depends on you to develop a healthful exercise program suitable for her age, stage of development, health, and physical abilities. Charm needs regular play sessions, exercise, and walks every day. Walking your Pom is good exercise for you, too!

As you plan Charm's exercise program, remember that all animals must first build up strength and endurance gradually. This requires a regular routine that, over time, may increase in length or vigor. Whatever you do, do not take Charm out for infrequent, strenuous exercise. This is especially hard on very young or very old Poms. Like all dogs (and people!), Charm must start with a moderate exercise program and build it up gradually to a level suitable for her age and health condition.

A regular exercise program will keep your Pom's heart healthy, build strong bones and joints, and develop muscles and muscle tone. Before you start Charm's exercise program, ask your veterinarian for exercise activity recommendations tailored to her needs and abilities.

Walking

Walking is great exercise. But when it comes to Poms, they seem to have two speeds: fast and faster. Young Poms love to do things at full speed, especially Pom pups. They have short bursts of energy and play hard for a brief period. Then they need long rest periods between play sessions. It is up to you to use good judgment when you walk your pet. Pom puppies less than one year of age and Pom adults more than seven years old should take it easy, whether they know it or not. They should not be forced to go on long walks. Their walks should be limited to short distances at a slow to casual pace, with long rest periods in between walks. The same is true for very old or overweight Poms. *Plan your Pom's walks according to her age and abilities. Make sure your Pom does not overexert!*

Do not walk your Pom in hot weather. Poms are Nordic dogs that are not adapted to warm weather. Your Pom could quickly overheat on a warm day during exercise and even suffer from heatstroke. In the summer, or when days are warm, walk your Pom in the early morning or evening hours when the weather is cooler.

Start with short walks each day and *gradually* increase the distance. Charm's natural pace is different from your own. It is much quicker, and she has to take a lot of steps to equal one of your strides. Watch Charm closely for signs of fatigue. Slow down to accommodate her and carry her if she is tired. If she overexerts, she can develop muscle spasms and lameness.

Whenever possible, let Charm exercise and play on soft surfaces, such as lawns or sandy beaches. Rocky or gravel surfaces are hard on your pet's tiny feet. Sidewalks and asphalt are uncomfortable and hard on the joints. They are also very hot a few inches above the ground, at Pom level. Be sure to check Charm's feet for stickers, torn toenails, cuts, or abrasions at the end of every walk. If Charm develops foot sores, treat them and discontinue the walks until the lesions have completely healed. If you live in an area with snow, do not walk Charm on salted roadways, and be

Tea Solution for Tender Feet

Here is a formula that you can mix and *apply* to your Pomeranian's feet to help toughen foot pads and dry sore lesions. *Do not allow your pet to drink this solution!*

1. Boil 2 cups (500 ml) of water.
2. Steep 10 orange pekoe black tea bags in the water for 20 minutes.
3. Crush 10 aspirin tablets (325 mg tablets) and dissolve them in the tea solution.
4. Allow the mixture to cool before using.
5. Apply solution to affected areas of the foot pads 3 to 4 times daily until lesions are healed. If the lesions are raw or open, omit aspirin from the solution.
6. This solution will keep for several months when stored in a tightly closed jar.

sure to rinse her feet after each walk so she doesn't develop salt burns.

Whenever possible, walk on level surfaces, especially if Charm is young and still in her developmental growth phase, or if she is older, or suffering from arthritis. Climbing hills and stairs is hard on growing bones and joints or aged hips and shoulder joints. Exercise should be fun and beneficial. It should not be stressful or cause injury or pain.

Swimming

Swimming is a good form of exercise—for dogs such as Labradors! But

Poms love to play fetch and they're good at it, too!

swimming is not such a good idea for Pomeranians unless it is in the form of therapeutic, supervised hydrotherapy.

Pools, lakes, and oceans are cold, and a small Pom can chill very easily after a short time in the water. Besides, chlorinated pool water and salty ocean water can damage a Pom's beautiful coat.

If your Pom goes swimming, rinse the chlorine or saltwater from her hair, dry her thoroughly, keep her warm, and brush her very well. Make sure her eyes are not irritated and her ears are completely dry.

Never leave your Pomeranian unattended in the water.

Fetch

Pomeranians are great at playing fetch. You can use lots of interesting objects for this game, including balls, dumbbells, and soft stuffed toys. Do not use hard toys or toys with sharp edges that could injure your Pom's mouth and teeth.

Tracking Games

Pomeranians have a keen sense of smell. Tracking is an interesting game for Poms. Just hide little tidbits around the house or yard for her to find. If Charm seems to have a natural ability for this game, consider contacting the American Kennel Club for a Tracking Regulations brochure. Pomeranians are very bright and can do just about anything. Your Pom may enjoy earning a Tracking Dog title!

Toys

Pomeranians love their toys and can be quite possessive of them. Teach children not to try to take toys away from your pet. A very possessive Pom can bite!

No matter what toys you buy, plan for them to end up as chew toys, whether designed for that purpose or not. Always be sure that the toys you buy are durable and safe.

Exercise Reminders
• Always keep your Pomeranian on a leash when you are exercising her in public. This act of responsible dog ownership will greatly reduce the chances of loss or injury.
• Be sensitive to your dog's needs. If she is panting and having difficulty keeping up, stop exercising immediately! She may suffer from overexertion or heatstroke.

Toys to Avoid

Dangerous Toys	Risks
Rawhide bones	Knots of rawhide or other shapes can obstruct the trachea and gastrointestinal tract
Latex toys, rubber toys, cotton ropes, hard plastic toys	May shred or break and obstruct the gastrointestinal tract
Toys small enough to be swallowed	May obstruct trachea or gastrointestinal tract

Chew toys are great for stimulating the gums and exercising the jaws. They help to pass the time and prevent boredom when you are not home. Some chew toys help reduce tartar buildup on the teeth. Chew toys are useful tools to help keep Charm from chewing on valuables, such as furniture or clothing. Never give Charm an old shoe or piece of clothing as a chew toy. She will not know the difference between an old, discarded item and your most expensive clothing or shoes. By allowing Charm to chew on old shoes, you are telling her that anything in your closet is fair game. Do not confuse her!

Not all toys are suitable for Pomeranians. For example, cow hooves, available as chew toys in local pet stores, are hard and can cause tooth fracture. Other toys, including rawhide bones, may break, shred, or tear and become lodged in the airway passages or gastrointestinal tract.

The best toys are those that cannot break or shred, are too big to be swallowed, and can also provide dental prophylaxis by gum stimulation and removing tartar buildup on the teeth.

Select toys for Charm based on the kind of dog she is. Some Pomeranians are very gentle with their toys and would never try to tear them apart. They love soft stuffed toys. Other Poms are more interested in finding out what is inside of every toy they own, so they need tough, durable toys.

Children and Pomeranians

The Pomeranian's appeal spans all age ranges. Children are drawn to the Pomeranian for its endearing appearance and its toy size. But children must be taught that Poms are real dogs, not toys. Children must respect these spunky, independent, bold dogs and resist the temptation to touch them until given permission to do so.

Pomeranians are outgoing, social, and protective of their owners. They need time to become acquainted with strangers and can be very wary of them. Every Pomeranian is different.

Some are very friendly, others resent intrusions. Like all dogs, Pomeranians can bite if they are startled or if they feel that they, or their owners, are threatened.

Pomeranians are not suitable pets for very small children. Small children can be flighty and noisy and frighten a Pom. Even though they are small, children can also seriously injure a tiny Pom by picking it up by a limb, or by the nape of the neck and dropping it. Pomeranian bones are delicate and can fracture easily, even when the fall is a short one. The dangers do not end here. A Pomeranian in pain can inflict serious bite wounds. Small children's heads are large in proportion to their bodies, and they often place their faces near animals when they play. The majority of animal bite wounds inflicted on children, regardless of animal species, happen in the area of the face and head.

Children in the family, of any age, must be taught to approach the new arrival quietly and gently until she is adapted to her new situation and knows all the family members. To prevent accidents, teach children not to pet or handle your Pom unless they have permission, are under adult supervision, and are seated. Supervision is always necessary when a child is caressing any dog of any breed.

With adult guidance, children can learn a lot from a Pomeranian. These wonderful dogs provide an excellent opportunity for adults to teach children about pets, the importance of humane care and treatment, kindness, and respect for life. They provide a way for children to learn responsibility by participating in the animal's care, learning the importance of fresh water, good food, a clean home, and a kind heart. Just be sure that you never count on the children to take care of your Pom. Children are forgetful and irresponsible! *Your Pomeranian's care is your job!*

Some children are frightened or uncomfortable around dogs, especially large ones. Because a Pomeranian is small and appealing, it can make it possible for a child to replace anxiety, fear, or timidity with tenderness and affection.

Even children who are somewhat shy will often talk freely when they are in the presence of animals. While watching a Pomeranian at play, or taking it on a walk, you and a child can share thoughts about the importance of animals in our lives.

Your Pom may influence children a lot more than you know at the time. She can be a dear friend and companion. In the process, a child can learn a lot about other Pomeranian-related things, such as animal behavior, training, exhibiting, and grooming. Your Pom just might influence a child to become a serious future Pomeranian fancier. After all, some of today's children are tomorrow's Pomeranian breeders!

Chapter Six

On the Go! Traveling with Your Pomeranian

Pomeranians love to travel, and no doubt, a big part of the reason you chose this toy breed is because of its small, portable size. Surely you are planning on taking your Pom with you wherever and whenever you can. Whether you are exhibiting at dog shows, running errands in the neighborhood, taking a vacation, or traveling the globe, your Pom wants to go with you!

A well-mannered Pomeranian makes a wonderful ambassador for the breed and is a big crowd pleaser. Your social canine will love the attention he receives from all his admirers and you will love having his company. Having your Pom as a traveling companion makes it much more fun to take a trip. So, a detailed discussion on travel and some useful travel tips are in order.

Travel Tips

1. Train your Pomeranian to a travel kennel. Make sure Max feels comfortable and secure inside it. This training begins early in life, by using the travel crate daily. Put food tidbits and toys in the crate to make it more inviting. When it comes time to travel, your Pom will feel at home in his travel crate and will not be stressed or frightened.

2. Make a few short practice trips, even if it is just driving around the block.

3. Make hotel, campground, and airline reservations well in advance and *be sure to tell them you are traveling with a dog.*

4. Make a list of everything you will need and pack early.

5. Microchip your Pomeranian and buy identification tags for the collar and harness.

6. Obtain a health certificate for out-of-state or international travel within ten days of your departure date. Your Pom should be in excellent health and able to make the trip. Schedule an appointment with your veterinarian to make sure vaccines are up to date. Ask if special medications for the trip are recommended, such as medication for the prevention of heartworm disease or car sickness.

7. Make sure you have all the things you will need during the trip, including items in case of illness or emergency.

Travel Supplies

- Travel kennel
- Collar with identification tag and leash
- Dishes, food, and bottled water
- Medications
- First aid kit
- Toys and bedding
- Grooming supplies
- Cleanup equipment: pooper scooper, plastic bags, paper towels, and carpet cleaner
- Veterinary records and photo identification

On the Road Again! Traveling by Car

Pomeranians enjoy car travel. Some dogs, especially puppies, can become carsick on their first few trips.

Warning!

Never leave your Pomeranian in a parked car on a hot day, even for a few minutes. Your Pomeranian cannot tolerate hot weather. The temperature inside a car, even with the windows cracked open and parked in the shade, can quickly soar past 120°F (49°C) within a few short minutes, and your small Pom can rapidly die of heatstroke.

To reduce the likelihood that Max will be carsick, limit his food and water two hours before travel begins and, if possible, place his crate where he can see outside of the car.

Tranquilizers are not always effective in preventing carsickness. An option you can discuss with your veterinarian is the use of an antihistamine (Antivert, meclizine) that has been shown to be effective for some dogs. But the best thing is to simply train your Pom so that he becomes accustomed to car travel.

Most dogs develop carsickness because they are apprehensive about car travel. A good way to help your pet overcome travel anxiety is to put his favorite toy in his travel crate with him and take him on a short car trip around the block. When you return home, immediately praise him and give him a food reward. Repeat this daily and your Pom will stop worrying about traveling and instead look forward to the next car adventure.

Make sure your Pom has a water dish secured inside of the travel crate.

Take to the Skies!
Flying with Your Pom

Your Pom's portable size makes it easy for you to take him on domestic flights. Max may be small enough to board the plane as a carry-on and fit comfortably under the seat in front of you in his travel crate. If your Pom is flying with you in the cabin, you will have to take him out of his crate and hold him when the crate is X-rayed at the security checkpoint. Otherwise, the airlines and airport officials mandate that your pet remain in his travel carrier at all times.

Your Pom must be able to sit, stand, turn around, and lie down comfortably in his travel crate. If the crate is too large to fit under the seat in front of you, your pet will travel in the cargo area while you travel in the cabin. Do not worry about Max if he is assigned to the cargo section of the airplane. The cargo area is pressurized and temperature contolled, just like the cabin of the plane. Nevertheless, it is always more fun and less worrisome if your Pom can travel in the cabin with you, and it is less expensive. If a Pom travels with its owner in the cabin, the cost is the same as for one piece of excess luggage. This is about one-sixth the cost of the dog's airfare if it flies in the belly of the plane in the cargo area.

Most airlines allow only two animals in the cabin and also limit the number of animals allowed in cargo for each flight, so make your reservation as soon as possible. With heightened security, airlines now change their shipping regu-

If your Poms travel together, make sure their crate is large enough to accommodate them. Because of their heavy coats and high metabolism, Poms can quickly overheat inside a crate that is too small or overcrowded. These Poms definitely need more room!

lations and required documentation often, depending on current events as well as weather conditions. Check with the airlines before you make reservations. Ask the airline company what its specific requirements are so that you will be prepared *before* you arrive at the airport.

Overseas travel is different. Most airlines will not allow pets in the cabin for overseas flights. There are also special requirements for dogs entering foreign countries, so check with the airlines as well as the embassies of the countries you will be visiting to be sure all the necessary requirements and documentation are in order.

Keep your Pom hydrated during the trip. If he travels in the cabin with you, bring a small dish, or a portable

Cool, Clear Water! Keep Your Pom Hydrated During Travel

Poms can quickly become dehydrated. It is extremely important that your Pom have as much water as he wants during the flight. Of course, water will spill out of the water dish while the crate is being transported and loaded on the plane. No one will be there to refill the water dish, but there is a simple solution that works. (This author knows from personal experience, having shipped numerous dogs overseas, with all of them arriving at their destinations with plenty of water remaining to drink!)

1. Train your Pomeranian to use a water bottle with a sipper tube.

2. Buy a plastic water dish that can be secured to the inside of the travel crate door.

3. Buy a large water bottle with sipper tube that attaches to the outside of the travel crate door. The flat, square Lixit brand water bottle that holds 32 ounces (960 ml) and is designed for this purpose is highly recommended.

4. Fill the water dish with water and freeze it the night before the flight.

5. Immediately before leaving for the airport, take the water dish containing the ice out of the freezer and attach the dish to the inside of the travel crate door.

6. Securely attach the full water bottle to the outside of the crate door. Place the sipper tube high enough that your Pom can comfortably drink from it, and situate the sipper tube directly above the plastic water dish.

Because the dish contains ice, water will not slop out of it during travel to the airport, checking in, and loading on the plane. Your Pom can drink from the water dish as the ice slowly thaws, or she can drink from the water bottle. If the water bottle drips during jostling, the dripped water will fall into the dish below the sipper tube and prevent water loss during travel. During the flight, your Pom can drink from either the water bottle or the dish and little, if any, water will be lost from spillage.

These steps will help to create a pleasant travel experience for your Pom.

folding dish, and offer him water frequently. Train your Pom to drink out of a sports bottle or a water bottle with a sipper tube, and offer him water throughout the trip. It is important that your Pom learn how to use a water bottle *before* he travels.

Tranquilizers are not necessary for air travel. In fact, tranquilizers can be harmful for dogs during travel and at high altitude can cause serious problems, including death. Poms that are used to traveling in their crates—whether by ground, air, or sea—usually settle in comfortably for the trip and fall right to sleep after takeoff. Your pet will probably sleep better on the trip than you will!

Chapter Seven

Picture Perfect: Grooming Your Pomeranian

A beautiful Pomeranian has the power to stop people in their tracks—and then steal their hearts! Poms are crowd pleasers, and wherever you go with your diminutive Spitz, she will attract lots of admirers and love being the center of attention. A big part of your Pom's luring appeal is her stunning, plush, stand-off, double coat. This beautiful dense coat was not created overnight. It is the result of your hard work and dedicated efforts to give your Pom everything she needs to grow a gorgeous gown: good nutrition, excellent health care, and thorough grooming. Regular grooming keeps the skin healthy, distributes natural oils in the coat, and keeps it free of mats. Grooming is an essential part of Charm's health care. Whether you are preparing for the show ring or for a walk in the park, your Pom should always look like a winner!

Coat Quality

Your Pomeranian inherited her coat quality, density, texture, and color from her parents. Without the genes necessary to grow a fabulous show coat, all the products in the world (shampoos, rinses, nutritional supplements, brushes, and combs) will not turn an ordinary coat into a champion show coat. There is no substitute for good genetics that can be purchased in a bottle at the pet store. A beautiful coat starts by buying a healthy, high-quality Pomeranian with an excellent pedigree from a reputable breeder. Then it is up to you to make sure your Pom coats up to her full genetic potential by giving her the best food and care that you possibly can.

Nutrition plays a major role in coat quality. Research has shown that 30 percent of the protein in a dog's diet is used to support the skin and coat. For a densely coated breed, such as the Pomeranian, the percentage may be even higher.

Many skin and hair problems are caused by poor diet, inadequate nutrition, junk foods, or food allergies. *A Pomeranian that does not receive the right kind of high-quality food and a*

It's not easy to grow a beautiful coat. It requires regular grooming, high quality nutrition, and the right genetics.

balanced diet can never grow a beautiful coat.

Too often Pom owners spend a fortune on vitamin supplements and hair products, when what they really need to do is buy better dog food. When it comes to nutrition, do not cut corners. Your Pom's total health depends on her nourishment. Good nutrition will keep your Pom healthy and produce a glorious coat. And in the long run you will save money on veterinary care, supplements, products, and medication by simply investing a little bit more in a high-quality food.

Your Pom's coat mirrors her health status. If she has parasites, allergies, hormonal problems, or is sick, the problems will be reflected in her coat's poor appearance.

Skin

Healthy skin is absolutely necessary to grow beautiful hair. We often just think about the hair, because the skin is obscured underneath it all, but it is skin health that determines whether a thick, full coat can grow. Skin is the largest organ of the body, covering its entire surface. Clearly, skin care is a very important part of grooming and health care.

Protect the skin.

1. Do not use harsh shampoos, chemicals, or products on your Pom's skin.

2. Avoid hot, dry environments that can dry out your pet's skin. It is not unusual for Pomeranians to develop itchy, flaky skin during the winter if they are subjected to the drying effects of heaters, radiators, and fireplaces.

3. Protect your Pom from unsanitary and damp environments that can cause skin problems such as bacterial and fungal infections.

Prevent skin allergies.

1. Feed your Pom a high-quality diet. If she has food allergies, feed her a hypoallergenic diet. Ask your veterinarian for recommendations.

2. Give your Pom bedding made of cotton or wool. Synthetic bedding, such as nylon or rayon, and beds containing cedar shavings, can cause skin allergies.

3. Check regularly for parasites and treat them immediately before they get out of control. Flea allergy dermatitis (FAD) is one of the leading causes of hair loss in dogs. It takes only a few flea bites to cause an allergic flare-up over the entire body.

Hair Growth

Your Pomeranian's hair does not grow continuously. Dog hair grows in cycles. The active growth cycle is called the *anagen phase*. The resting phase, when hair is retained in the hair follicle as dead hair, is called the *telogen phase*. The *catagen phase* is a transitional period leading to the telogen phase.

Hair is made up of almost solid protein, called *keratin*. So it makes sense that a balanced diet containing high-quality, digestible protein is essential for growing a beautiful coat. A single dog hair in the anagen phase may grow only .1 to .2 mm each day, but if you multiply that distance by the hundreds of thousands of growing hairs on Charm's body, it can total more than 50 feet (15 m) of hair growth each day! If your Pomeranian is in poor health or receives an inadequate diet, hair growth can be shortened, delayed, or halted. The hair cuticle can be faulty and the hair will be dull, lack luster, and break.

Hormonal imbalances can also cause hair loss or skin problems. Growth hormone dermatosis/sex hormone dermatosis alopecia X is a common problem in Poms that causes hair loss and skin problems. Hypothyroidism also causes skin problems and hair loss. In addition, normal hormonal

A thick, plush coat takes time to grow and even more time to maintain. A Pom's coat is a lot of work and requires frequent grooming.

changes after giving birth cause mother Poms to shed out most of their coat. This is called *postpartum effluvium*, and although it sounds scary and looks unattractive, the hair loss is normal and temporary and the hair eventually grows back. Unfortunately, postpartum effluvium usually is most apparent at six to eight weeks after giving birth—very inconveniently about the same time potential puppy buyers ask to see the mother of the pups! Just when the breeder would like to show off the mother looking her loveliest, mother Pom will often have shed much of her coat and look a bit scraggily.

Shedding and Photoperiod

Poms are housed indoors, so they shed year-round, rather than seasonally. This is because the photoperiod, or number of hours of daylight exposure each day, affects shedding more than environmental temperature does. Photoperiod is an important factor in the lives of most species and affects many biological processes, including shedding, reproduction, sleep cycles, melanin production, and changes in pigmentation.

Pomeranians are usually exposed to several hours of light year-round, because they live indoors and are exposed to artificial lighting, even in winter when there are fewer hours of sunlight. Although hair is shed throughout the year, not all of it is shed at one time. On your Pomeranian's body, different hairs are in different stages of growth. Poms typically shed in a mosaic pattern throughout the body. For this reason, daily brushing is very important to remove dead hairs, stimulate the skin, and distribute natural oils in the coat.

Grooming Is Fun!

Grooming your Pomeranian is hard work, but it is also a lot of fun! It is a way for you and Charm to enjoy each other's company and strengthen your bond of friendship. Many Pom owners groom their dogs as a form of relaxation. It is a known fact that people can lower their blood pressure simply by touching or caressing an animal, so just imagine what a nice grooming session can do for both you and your Pom! Charm will enjoy the attention and skin stimulation and feel better after a good brushing. And you will have no doubt when you watch her prance about that she *knows* she looks terrific, too.

Grooming is not just for cosmetic purposes. All Pomeranians need to be combed, brushed, and bathed routinely to keep their coats healthy, shiny, and free of mats. If the coat becomes matted, its insulating quality will be lost. Mats are good hiding places for parasites, such as fleas, ticks, and mites. Because severely matted hair cannot be untangled, you will have to cut them out with scissors, and this will make your companion look uneven and ragged. By regularly brushing and bathing Charm, you can observe her overall appearance and condition on a daily basis by checking the skin, eyes, ears, teeth, and nails. You can detect signs of problems (irritated, tearing eyes; foul-smelling ears; lumps, parasites, and sores) early, before they become a serious health problem.

If you do not have the time or do not want to groom your Pom, then a Pomeranian is not the dog for you. It is true that you can hire a professional groomer, but remember that for a beautiful coat, your Pom needs daily brushing. Also, professional grooming requires time and money. Even if you take Charm to a groomer on a regular basis—a minimum of once every three weeks is recommended—she still needs daily brushing to keep her coat healthy and free of mats. So if you love your Pom, you must also learn to love to groom her. If Charm is well trained and used to being groomed, you will discover that grooming her is an absolute pleasure and that the results are well worth your time and effort.

Learn to Love Grooming

Both you and your Pom will learn to love grooming. Your Pom puppy is young enough that learning to be groomed can be a fun game for her. And learning how to groom can be a rewarding experience for you!

Do not wait until Charm is an adolescent with a mind of her own before you begin training her. Begin training immediately, while she is still a puppy. Charm may protest or object to brushes and combs in the beginning. In fact, Poms can be very vocal and quite dramatic. Remain calm and do not baby your Pom. Simply speak to her reassuringly and reward her with praise when she allows you to brush her. Charm will quickly learn to accept daily hair care, especially if you give her lots of praise and keep grooming sessions short. By grooming every day you also prevent problem mats and knots from forming, so grooming is much easier.

Always end grooming sessions before your Pom tires of them and starts to misbehave. If Charm objects and struggles and you stop grooming, she will have accomplished her goal: to make you stop grooming. You will only have reinforced her bad behavior by giving her the impression that if she does not cooperate, you will do as she wants and stop grooming. Poms can be stubborn, so Charm must learn that you are the one in charge. Be gentle, kind, consistent, yet firm, and always end grooming sessions with lots of praise and a small, healthful food treat.

Training Tips to Prepare Your Pom Puppy for Grooming:

1. Take your Pom out for a walk or play with her in the backyard so she can eliminate and then burn up some energy playing. If Charm is a bit tired before you begin grooming, she may be less inclined to resist or protest.

2. Prepare your Pomeranian for the type of handling she will receive during grooming. Begin by placing her on your lap and caressing her head, face, and ears in a soothing, calming manner, then handle each of her feet. Make it a pleasant experience.

Let your Pom play in the yard before each grooming session.

3. Gently place a brush on Charm's back. At first she will try to examine the object or chew on it. Once the curiosity has passed, try to gently brush her back. As your puppy accepts this contact, gently and lightly brush the top of her head, her legs, and her tail.

4. In between brushing, rub her belly and scratch her ears.

5. Keep the first training sessions very short. Three to five minutes is long enough. Stop while Charm is enjoying the attention and wants more.

6. Give a small food reward to let Charm know she was good and to signal that the grooming session has ended.

Table Training Your Pom

Ideally, the breeder will have introduced Charm to a grooming table early in puppyhood, as soon as she had a little bit of hair to fluff and buff. If Charm is still a puppy, you can pick up on table training where the breeder left off.

A grooming table allows you to work in various positions at a comfortable level, without bending or stooping. Before you can safely groom Charm on a table, she must learn to sit, lie down, and stand still on it. Most important, she must learn not to jump off the table.

Never leave your Pomeranian unattended on the grooming table, no matter how well you think she is trained or how much you trust her. If your Pom jumps or falls from the table, she can be seriously injured.

Place a rubber nonslip mat on the tabletop. In the beginning you can let your puppy sit, stand, or lie down. The main thing at this point is for her simply to remain on the table and keep reasonably still so that you can gently brush or comb her. Later, as Charm has more training, you can ask her to change her position to make it easier to reach and groom different parts of her coat.

• Learning to sit on the grooming table: First say your pet's name to get her attention. Then say, "*Sit.*" Use a small treat to hold just above Charm's head. As her nose points up toward the treat, her rump will drop down. Gently push or hold her bottom down on the table and repeat the word *sit*. Restrain your Pom for a few seconds in the sitting position. Give lots of praise and a food reward. Repeat this a few times, always saying your pet's name, then the word *sit*. Give Charm time to sit on her own without your placing or holding her in the sit position. If she does not sit right away, then show her what you want her to do. Keep training sessions short, no more than three minutes. After a few sessions, Charm will learn to pay attention when you say her name and will make the association between the word "sit" and the action. At the end of each training session, take Charm off the table, give her a small food reward, and cuddle her. This is your way of letting her know that she did a great job and that her time on the table has ended.

• Learning to stand on the grooming table: Several lessons later, when Charm knows how to sit on the table, you can teach her to stand on it. First say your pet's name, then give the command *stand*. Hold her gently with one hand supporting underneath her chest and one hand under her belly, and repeat the word *stand*. If Charm tries to sit down, say her name and then say, "*Stand.*" If she ignores you, gently support her underside so she must stand. Make these first training sessions short, no longer than five minutes. When you are finished, give Charm lots of praise and a small food reward, take her off the table, and snuggle with her.

• Learning to lie down on the grooming table: Begin by saying your Pom's name to get her attention and showing her a food reward. Say, "*Down.*" When she does not respond, slowly lower the food to the table surface. This should encourage Charm to lie down to reach the food, but in the beginning you may have to apply light pressure to the top of her shoulders or pull one leg gently out in front of her. When Charm is in the down position, praise her and give her the food reward. As with other commands, you will eventually replace the food reward with praise alone. After Charm has learned to lie down on her belly, you will teach her to lie on her sides so you can groom her. Begin by placing Charm on her side. If she struggles, hold her in

Brush your Pom daily to remove shedding hair, stimulate the skin, and spread natural oils throughout the coat.

Once your pet is accustomed to lying, sitting, or standing on the grooming table; knows her commands, and remains still without trying to jump off the table, you can begin training her to be handled, brushed, and combed.

Begin by gently lifting and holding each foot for a few seconds. As Charm becomes used to having her feet handled, you can hold each foot for longer periods of time and handle each toe individually, as you will have to do later when you trim the toenails. Gently handle the ears, face, body, and tail. When your Pomeranian accepts your handling calmly and remains on the table, you can introduce her to a soft brush and begin gently grooming her. At this point do not worry about brushing every hair. Simply focus on getting your pet used to being brushed while on the table. Limit this training session to two or three minutes. That is a long time for a Pom puppy! Give Charm lots of praise and a small food reward, take her off the table, and hold her when training has ended.

During the next training session, use a spray bottle filled with water and lightly spray the coat. At first, the spray bottle may startle Charm. Spend a little extra time reassuring her so she becomes accustomed to the sound and sensation of the spray.

Continue to accustom your puppy to objects touching her body. Place the brush lightly on Charm's back and sides and then begin to gently brush the surface of the coat. Do not worry about her face and ears right now. If Charm

position firmly but gently. Charm will probably try to get up. Most Pomeranians resist being placed on their backs or sides because this is a subordinate position and they feel vulnerable. Hold gently until your puppy has stopped squirming. If she protests, speak to her reassuringly, but continue to firmly hold her on her side. Keep these sessions short and give your Pom a food reward. Then take her off the table, praise her, and hold her.

Do not try to teach your Pomeranian all three commands—sit, stand, and down—in one session. Teach your Pom one position at a time over several lessons and let her learn each command well before teaching her a new one.

seems to enjoy the massage, continue for a few more minutes. Be sure to stop before your puppy tires of it. If you are training a very young animal, remember that they bore easily, and limit sessions to three to five minutes.

Pomeranians have very sensitive skin, especially baby Poms. Be gentle and patient. Do your best to make the training experience a pleasant one. If Charm learns to associate the grooming table with enjoyment, she will be cooperative, and grooming sessions will be much easier and more fun for both of you.

Grooming Tools and Supplies

Have all of your supplies handy before you begin:
- Grooming table
- Nonslip mat and towels
- Brush with flexible pins or natural bristle
- Fine slicker brush, or small curved slicker brush
- Comb with rotating pins, teeth spaced close together (for fine hair)
- Comb with rotating pins, teeth spaced farther apart (for coarse hair)
- Flea comb
- Scissors (blunt tipped)
- Thinning shears
- Nail trimmers
- Styptic powder or gel
- Spray bottle
- Emollient shampoo (pH balanced for dog skin)
- Gentle hair rinse (developed for dogs)

- Ear cleaning solution (available from your veterinarian)
- Cotton-tipped swabs or cotton balls
- Paper towels
- Soft washcloths
- Hair dryer
- Electric nail grinder (optional)

Grooming to Perfection

Now that Charm is trained to the grooming table and familiar with grooming tools and handling, it is time to get serious about grooming. Whether you plan to show off your pet in the neighborhood or in the show ring, her glamorous coat will attract admirers like a magnet. Of course, if your Pom is competing at the shows, there may be times when you hire a professional groomer and handler so you can sit back and admire your Pom strut her stuff, but for the most part, the credit for her regal appearance will all go to you.

Pomeranian owners develop their own individual grooming methods that work best for them and give them the results they desire. You can master the art of grooming your Pom to perfection after many hours of practice. You can also learn helpful tips from accomplished Pomeranian breeders, handlers, and groomers.
- Start by spraying your Pom lightly with water and a small amount of gentle hair rinse or crème conditioner designed for canines. Brushing or combing dry hair will cause the hair to break.

- Brush from the top of the coat all the way to the skin.
- Be gentle! Pomeranian skin is sensitive!
- Brush the neck, back, sides, underbelly, legs, and tail.
- Pay particular attention to the axillary region (under the armpit area), groin area (inside of thighs), belly, behind and at the base of the ears, and under the tail. These problem areas tend to become matted or soiled and are often overlooked.
- Using a slicker brush, gently brush Charm's coat. Brush the coat in sections and *in layers*, so that no part of the coat surface or depth is missed.
- When the coat has been thoroughly brushed, change to a wide-toothed comb to gently work out tangles, especially on the chest and flank.
- Check the undercoat for mats and carefully remove them with scissors.
- Be careful around the base of the ears, where knots form easily. If you cannot comb out the knots and must cut them out, be very careful not to accidentally cut the skin, that adheres tightly to the knots.
- For final touch ups, use a fine-toothed comb.
- Trim away stray hairs from the tops of the ears to make the ears look small, neat, and *rounded*. Be very careful not to cut the ears!
- Carefully trim away hair under the tail and around the anus with thinning scissors to help keep the area clean.
- Be very careful when trimming around the genital area.
- Brush the legs well and trim stray hairs from the hocks and pasterns.

- Using blunt-tipped scissors, trim excess hair away from foot pads and between the toes. Trim away little tufts of hair on the top of the feet.
- When the entire coat is completely groomed down to the skin and is free of tangles and mats, brush the hair on the neck, shoulders, chest, and body against the direction of growth to give the appearance of a large mane or rough and to make the coat stand up and out from the body, giving it volume.
- Brush the tail and trim away stray hairs, so that the tail rests like a beautiful large plumed fan on your Pom's back.

Check for Problems

Grooming sessions are the perfect time to thoroughly inspect your pet's skin to be sure she is healthy and to check for signs of dry or oily skin, lumps and bumps, parasites, stickers, scabs, knots, and mats.

Summer Trim

If your Pom's coat is too heavy for summer and too much work for you, ask your groomer to thin, trim, and shape the coat. Your groomer can give your Pom a darling do for the summer that requires less maintenance. Just do not ask to have your Pom's coat clipped short to the skin. When clipped short, the outer coat may not return to its natural length, texture, and appearance and your Pom may lose her classic Nordic chic look.

Gently wipe around your Pom's eyes with a soft, damp cloth to remove small particles and stains.

Check your Pom's eyes. They should be clear and bright and free of discharge. If Charm's eyes frequently tear, contact your veterinarian. Prolonged tearing can stain the hair around the inner corners of the eyes. Your veterinarian can provide you with a product developed specifically for use around the eyes that can help eliminate the stain. More important, your veterinarian can determine the cause of tearing and treat it appropriately, before it becomes a serious problem. If your Pom has an eye problem, do not use products prescribed for yourself or for your other pets, and do not use drops or ointments containing corticosteroids unless your veterinarian has specifically prescribed them for your Pom's current eye condition. *If your Pomeranian is squinting, has reddened scleras (the whites of the eyes), pale blue areas on the surface of either or both eyes, is tearing, or has a discharge from the eyes, contact your veterinarian immediately.*

Be sure to check Charm's ears for dirt and wax buildup. The ears should be clean and free of discharge. Avoid ear-cleaning products containing alcohol unless your veterinarian has specifically recommended them. Alcohol is very drying and can be painful on raw, tender, or reddened areas. If you detect a foul odor or discharge in the ears, contact your veterinarian. These could indicate a bacterial or fungal infection, parasites, or foreign

Grooming is a very important part of your Pom's health care. Pomeranians enjoy grooming and the attention they receive while being groomed. Be gentle! Poms have sensitive skin. Brush your Pom daily and have her professionally groomed on a regular basis to prevent mats from forming and to keep the skin healthy and the coat plush and beautiful.

bodies. Ear problems are very painful and can lead to hearing loss.

Anal Sacs

Express the anal sacs *before* you bathe your Pomeranian. Anal sacs are at either side of the inside of the rectum. They feel like tiny grapes and contain a foul-smelling, brown, liquid substance. If the sacs are not expressed, or emptied, on a regular basis, they can become impacted, infected, or abscessed and rupture.

How to express anal sacs

• Wear disposable gloves.
• Place an absorbent tissue over the anus to absorb the anal sac discharge.
• Feel for the anal sac through the perianal tissue on each side of the anus.
• Gently squeeze on the sacs from the outside of the anus, with your thumb and index finger, until they empty into the tissue. Anal sac contents are normally brown in color and may range in consistency from liquid to pasty.

If you do not want to express your Pom's anal sacs, your veterinarian or groomer can do this for you.

Attention to details!

1. Make sure the coat is brushed thoroughly and through to the skin.

2. Trim away stray hairs.

3. Trim excess hair from between the toes and foot pads with blunt-tipped scissors and trim around the feet to give them a tight, compact, rounded, arched appearance. Neat,

trimmed feet look pretty and prevent hairballs, dirt, foreign objects (such as grass awns and stickers), and excess moisture (leading to bacterial growth, moist dermatitis, and sores) from accumulating between the toes. Your Pomeranian will walk better and track less dirt and debris into your home.

4. Trim excess hair away from the groin area and under the tail with blunt-tipped scissors.

5. Trim the toenails (see "Toenails"). If your Pomeranian's dewclaws (vestigial digits where a "thumb" would be) have not been surgically removed, remember to trim those as well. If left untrimmed, they can snag and tear or grow into surrounding tissue.

6. Keep toenails at a reasonable length.

7. Brush your Pom's teeth at least once every week.

Every little detail adds to your Pom's beauty and overall impression. The more you practice, the more stunning your Pom will look!

Bathing Your Pomeranian

On average, you should bathe your Pomeranian at least once every three weeks. Some Pomeranians require a bath once a week. Use a pH-balanced shampoo developed for canines that is gentle on the skin. For frequent bathing, an emollient shampoo is recommended. An emollient does not contain soaps, rinses out easily, and is very gentle on a Pomeranian's deli-

Make sure the bath water is a comfortable temperature for your Pom, rinse her well and do not let her catch cold.

cate skin. Emollient shampoos can be purchased from your veterinarian or pet store.

Always brush your Pom thoroughly before you give her a bath. If you don't remove knots, tangles, and mats before the bath, they will become fixed in the coat when it gets wet and will be even more difficult to remove later.

Pomeranians fit easily inside most sinks or bathtubs. To prevent injury, make sure Charm does not bump into the faucets (a common accident). Also, be sure the water is set at a comfortable temperature *before* you put her in the sink or use the sprayer to rinse her. Place a hair trap over the drain to catch loose hairs and put a nonslip mat in the bottom of the sink.

If you have more than one Pomeranian, consider buying a tub made especially for dog grooming. These specially designed dog tubs have the advantage of being at a comfortable working height, complete with sprayers to rinse the coat and a place to arrange grooming products and tools.

Begin by mixing some emollient shampoo with some warm water so that the mixture is a comfortable temperature before you apply it to the coat. If your Pomeranian has a flea problem, begin by wetting the head and working down the body to the tip of the tail. When a dog is submerged in water, or the coat gets wet, fleas have a tendency to climb toward higher ground—in this case, the head. If you do not start by washing the head, you will find the fleas congregated around the eyes, ears, and muzzle shortly after you begin. By washing the head first, you can suds and rinse the fleas down the body and into the bathwater.

If your Pom does not have a flea problem, being by lathering the tail

Dry your Pom well and make sure she does not catch cold. Very young and very old Poms are especially sensitive to the cold and damp. Keep your Pom comfortable and warm until she is completely dry.

water over the coat, work it in, and rinse well. Gently squeeze as much water as possible out of the coat.

Keep Your Pom Warm and Dry!

After you bathe your Pomeranian, make sure she does not become chilled. Blot excess water from her coat with a towel, then wrap her in another thick, large towel and dry thoroughly. Dry the ears well with a soft, dry cloth. You can use a cotton-tipped swab to dry and clean the ear canals, but do not probe deeply or you could hurt the ears.

Hair Dryers

After you have blotted excess water from the coat, begin blow-drying with a hair dryer. You may use a dog hair dryer designed to attach to a cage, or a handheld dryer to give you more styling control.

A hair dryer can speed up grooming and produce beautiful results. While drying the coat, you can also inspect the skin as the dryer separates the hairs.

Begin by turning the dryer on a low setting and holding it away from your pet. If she is startled, talk to her soothingly until she calms down. When Charm is no longer bothered by the sound of the dryer, set the dryer to low and gently blow-dry the hair on the back. Eventually, Charm will get used to the hair dryer and you may use it on the sides, shoulders, and neck. Always make sure the setting is low and the temperature is not hot.

area first and working forward. Massage and lather the hind legs, back, belly, shoulder, front legs, and neck. Massage the hair against the direction of growth. Wash the coat well and rinse it thoroughly with warm (not hot) water. Make sure all shampoo is completely removed. Any residual shampoo in the coat can cause dryness and itching.

Lather around the base of the ears and sides of the face. Wash the face and ears carefully with a soft cloth and do not allow soap or water to get into the ears and eyes. Gently wipe debris away from your Pomeranian's eyes, from the inner corner of the eye downward and outward.

If necessary, give your pet a second wash. After the final rinse, pour a mixture of crème rinse and warm

If you use a hair dryer, make sure the setting is not too hot and does not burn your Pom's skin. Keep your Pom indoors until she is completely dry.

Dry the coat from the skin outward. To prevent skin burns, keep moving the direction of air and do not point the dryer on an area of skin for too long. Dry the hair against the direction of growth to better separate the hairs in layers. Using a hair dryer will make the coat appear more voluminous and allow it to stand out from the body.

No matter what kind of hair dryer you use, make sure the air is not hot and does not dry or burn the skin.

The time and effort you invest in your Pomeranian's coat and skin will keep her looking in top condition. As you become more familiar with the Pomeranian standard and develop more skill at grooming, you will find ways to groom your dog so that you can enhance her features to more closely reflect the ideal Pomeranian and bring out her best.

Toenails

Unlike hair that grows in phases, toenails grow continuously. Pomeranians need to have their toenails clipped regularly, usually once a month. Check the nails frequently and do not let them get too long. Overgrown nails can eventually deform the paws, interfere with movement, and impede a dog's ability to walk. In the most severe cases, overgrown toenails can curve under and pierce the foot pads.

Toenail trimming is something most dog owners dread, but it really is not difficult if your Pom is trained to stand on a table and let you handle her feet. *If you do not want to trim your Pom's nails, your veterinarian or groomer can do it for you.*

To determine if Charm needs a nail trim, stand her on the grooming table. None of the nails should touch the surface of the table. You will notice that each toenail curves and tapers into a point. If the toenail is not too dark in color, you will be able to see pink inside of the toenail, or the "quick." This is the blood supply, and just below it is the excess nail growth that you will remove. If the toenails are too dark to differentiate where the quick ends, you can illuminate the nail with a penlight to find the line of demarcation where the blood supply ends.

There are different types of nail trimmers. Most Pomeranian owners prefer the guillotine-style clippers for adult dogs and baby nail clippers, designed for humans, for puppy toe-

If your Pom has been trained to let you handle her feet, trimming nails should not be difficult. Look for the pink inside of the toenail. This is the blood supply. Trim away the tip of the nail where it curves and tapers to a point and where the blood supply does not extend.

nails. To use the guillotine-style clippers, place the toenail inside the metal loop, aligning the upper and lower blades with the area you wish to cut, and squeeze the clipper handles. Cut only the very tip of the toenail. If the nail is still too long, continue to remove the end of the nail carefully in small increments. If you accidentally cut too close, you can stop the bleeding by applying styptic powder or gel, available from pet stores and veterinarians. If you do not have styptic powder or gel, cornstarch may be helpful. You can also stop the bleeding by applying pressure to the nail with a clean cloth for five minutes.

When the blades of the nail trimmers become dull they should be replaced so they do not break, shred, or crack the nails. Electric toenail grinders are used to round off and smooth the nails after trimming.

Be sure to always praise your Pomeranian for her cooperation. Without it, nail trimming is virtually impossible!

Dental Care

Regular dental care and tooth brushing are very important aspects of your Pomeranian's health care program and should start in early puppyhood.

Puppies, like babies, are born without teeth. When Pomeranians reach four to six weeks of age, their deciduous teeth (baby teeth) start to erupt. At around four months, these twenty-eight temporary teeth begin to fall out and are replaced with forty-eight permanent teeth. During this time, Pom pups want to chew on everything. It is important to provide your puppy with lots of safe chew toys. By the time a Pomeranian is six months old, all of the adult teeth should be in place. However, some Poms' adult teeth come in slowly and are not all present in the mouth by this age.

Adult teeth must last a lifetime, so it is important to take good care of them by preventing plaque and tartar buildup and periodontal disease.

Plaque is a coating on the teeth caused by a combination of bacteria, saliva, and decaying food. As plaque builds up, a concrete-like substance called tartar develops, usually starting at the gum line. It is yellow to brown in color and can eventually spread to cover the entire tooth. Periodontal disease develops as bacteria infect the root of the tooth and cause erosion of the surrounding bone that secures the tooth. Eventually, the root is destroyed and the tooth falls out, or requires extraction. Periodontal disease causes more problems than bad breath, swollen, painful, bleeding gums, and tooth loss. The bacteria present in the mouth and gums can enter the bloodstream and grow on the heart valves, causing heart problems, or infect the kidneys and other organs of the body. Tooth loss and periodontal disease are very common in Pomeranians. Fortunately, both can be prevented by regular dental brushing.

Start dental brushing when your Pom is just a pup. Baby teeth are good for practice and training. Use a small, soft toothbrush and a small amount of pet toothpaste. Do not use human toothpaste. Many human products contain spearmint or peppermint or other substances that cause dogs to salivate (drool) profusely or upset their stomachs. Brush each tooth gently in a circular motion. By the time the adult teeth are in, Charm will be used to the daily routine.

Start with the upper front teeth (incisors), brushing down and away from the gum line, and proceed back to the premolars and molars on one side of the mouth. Brush in a gentle, circular motion. Repeat on the upper teeth on the opposite side of the mouth. Look for possible problem areas as you brush.

From the incisors, work back to the molars, brushing up and away from the gum line. Repeat on the lower teeth on the opposite side of the

mouth. Be patient. You can break the daily brushing into two sessions at the beginning. Spend about one minute on the upper teeth and then praise Charm for good behavior. Later in the day you can spend another one-minute time increment on the bottom teeth, followed by profuse praise.

Good home dental care is a necessity, but it is not a replacement for veterinary dental visits. Even with the best of care, most Pomeranians need routine professional dental cleaning and polishing. Your Pom should have her teeth examined at least once every year, and more often if necessary, especially if she has bad breath.

Bad breath is not normal for a dog. It usually indicates periodontal disease or other health problems. If your Pom has bad breath, contact your veterinarian right away.

Even if your Pom is not competing in the show ring, she will always be Best in Show at your house—so give her the pampering she deserves!

All smiles! Start dental care when your Pom is a pup and she will quickly learn to accept and even enjoy it.

Show Ring Ready Grooming Tips

Here are a few summary tips to make grooming sessions safe and enjoyable for you and your Pomeranian:

1. Remember that several short training sessions are better than one long one. Limit puppy grooming to three to five minutes. Pom pups have short attention spans and bore easily.

2. Begin grooming training as soon as possible. The day after you bring your Pom home is a perfect time to start.

3. Designate an area to use exclusively for grooming. This should be an easy-to-clean, convenient location, close to an electrical outlet for hair dryer, electric nail grinder, and vacuum cleaner.

4. Select a table that is high enough for you to work at a comfortable height, sitting or standing.

5. Make sure the table surface is nonslip, to prevent falls or injury.

6. When your Pomeranian requires a reprimand, use the word *no* consistently.

7. Never use your pet's name in connection with a reprimand.

8. Train by using positive reinforcements: praise or food rewards.

9. Do not scold and *never* use physical punishment. Pomeranians are very sensitive and their feelings are easily hurt.

10. Invest in the best. Purchase high-quality tools and equipment to reduce your chances of developing blisters, or sore wrists and arms from overexertion.

11. Place all the grooming items near the grooming table, within easy reach.

12. Use only products designed for dogs to ensure a pH balance for canine skin, including emollient shampoos, spray-on dry shampoos, or self-rinse shampoos.

13. Do not use products containing flea, tick, lice, and mite killers unless they are specifically recommended by your veterinarian. These products are harsh on sensitive Pomeranian skin and can be harmful for toy breeds, especially young puppies.

14. Always praise your Pom for good behavior. Give a food reward at the end of each grooming session and take her for a walk afterward whenever possible. She will associate grooming with other pleasant experiences and look forward to the next grooming session.

15. Never leave your Pom unattended on the grooming table.

Chapter Eight

Feeding Your Pomeranian

Feeding a nutritionally complete and balanced diet is one of the most important things you can do for your Pomeranian. Good nutrition is absolutely essential to ensure your Pom's health and longevity. Every aspect of your tiny toy's well-being—from a healthy heart to a beautiful coat—is determined by the quality and quantity of the food he eats.

Your Pom has special nutritional needs to fuel his fast metabolism. He also has a small stomach, so he must eat small meals—and several of them! His stomach is too small to hold enough food in a single meal to supply his daily caloric needs and support his activity level, especially if he is a young puppy, or very active. He must have a good balance of protein, fats, and carbohydrates to prevent hypoglycemia (low blood sugar)—a common problem in Pomeranians.

Your Pom's diet must be high quality, highly digestible, and energy dense to make every bite count. Whether Max is a growing puppy, an active adult, or a senior citizen, giving him the right diet makes all the difference in his health and lifespan.

In ancient times, your diminutive Spitz's Nordic ancestors survived on raw meat, plant material (often found in the stomach of prey), and whatever else they could find. With gradual domestication, their meals consisted of remains from the hunt, vegetables from the garden, and table scrap leftovers. With their random and varied diets, most of the nutritional bases were more or less covered.

Commercial dog food made its appearance when dry kibble became

Pom pups need small, frequent meals or they can suffer from low blood sugar.

A Pom's nutritional needs and diet depend on its age, life stage, and activity level.

popular during World War II and when meat was a scarce commodity. As consumer convenience became paramount in our ever-pressed-for-time society, we witnessed the evolution of TV dinners, microwave meals, and fast food restaurants. The dog food business was ready to capitalize on modern lifestyles, knowing that people who did not take time to cook for their families were unlikely to cook for the family dog. The convenience of commercial dog food was promoted through extensive advertising until it became commonplace. Today, the manufacture and sale of pet food exceeds $20 billion annually.

Life Stages and Dietary Changes

The important role good nutrition plays in a Pomeranian's life cannot be overemphasized. High-quality nutrition is the key to overall good health and a long life span. Fortunately, it is one aspect of Max's health care over which you have full control.

Always feed your Pom the best food you can. Never cut corners on good nutrition or try to save money by purchasing cheap, inferior dog foods. The price you pay for high-quality food for your companion will be far outweighed by your savings in his health care expenses and the joy of extending the quality and length of his life. Of course, as Max grows, develops, and eventually ages, his nutritional needs will vary, so his diet will also change throughout his life. For example, when he is a puppy, Max will need a puppy food that provides complete and balanced nutrition for growth and development. As he reaches adolescence, his dietary requirements may lessen or increase, according to his individual needs and activities. When Max is an adult, he will have greater nutritional requirements if he is active, doing obedience or agility work, on the show circuit, or being used for breeding purposes. If he is sedentary, he will require less food or he can become overweight. Finally, as Max ages, or if he becomes sick or is recovering from an illness, he will need a diet suited to his health condition and special needs. He may need a senior diet or a special diet for medical conditions, such as heart or kidney failure, or skin allergies. If Max has a medical problem, your veterinarian can give him an appropriate prescription diet.

Environment and genetics also influence a Pom's caloric requirements, ability to digest and metabolize certain foods, and ability to maintain a normal weight. If some of Max's family members have weight problems (if they are overweight or underweight), this may be an inherited tendency in his family lines. Ask the breeder about any genetic problems among his family members and consult with your veterinarian. Closely monitor your Pom's food consumption. If Max is over-weight, a high-fiber weight-reduction diet may be necessary.

Starting Off Right

When you first bring Max home, ask the breeder what he is currently eating and buy at least a two-week supply of the same food. Continue feeding the same diet until he has had a chance to adjust to the new family and home. A change in diet, especially a sudden change in diet and feeding schedules, during this important adaptation time can be very stressful for a Pom. It can cause stomach upset and diarrhea.

Take Max to your veterinarian within forty-eight hours of purchase for a physical examination and to plan a complete health care program. The first veterinary visit is an ideal time to discuss your Pom's specific nutritional requirements. If a change in diet is in order, make the change gradually by increasing the amount of the new diet, and decreasing the amount of the old diet, in small increments.

For each of Max's life stages, you should consult your veterinarian to learn which type of dog food would be most beneficial. The ideal nutrition for him today may not be suitable later in life. With increasing consumer awareness, dog food manufacturers strive to maintain a competitive edge and offer dog owners a large selection of dog foods from which to choose. For these reasons, nutrition will be an important topic of discussion each time you visit your veterinarian.

Deciphering Dog Food Labels

Today there are countless brands and types of commercial dog foods available. Most claim to be the best food for your pet—but the truth is, not every dog food is perfect for Poms. Your Pom needs a high-quality, energy-rich, highly digestible food.

Dog food comes in all sizes, colors, shapes, and consistencies (dry kibble, semimoist, and moist canned). The brands are packaged and named to look and sound more like food for humans than for dogs because the marketing is aimed at *you*, the consumer. But Max does not care about the color or brand of his food, nor whether it is nutritionally complete. He cares only how his meals taste and smell. Some Poms can be very picky about their food and may even prefer junk food or inferior dog food formulations to high-quality nutrition. This is because many tastes and smells that appeal to dogs are from food additives and artificial flavorings, rather than what really matters: nutrients. It is up to you to choose a nutritious food that your Pom will enjoy. Just as incorrect feeding can harm Max's health and prevent him from living up to his full potential, the best dog food in the world will not benefit Max if he refuses to eat it.

The best way to select high-quality dog food for Max is to consult with your veterinarian and Pomeranian breeders. Another way is to study the dog food labels and select a premium dog food that provides complete and balanced nutrition from high-quality protein sources. Be careful! Dog food labels are confusing and do not always give you the type of information you want. For precise details you must contact the food manufacturers directly.

Here are some definitions to help you decipher and interpret dog food labels.

Ingredients

Ingredients include everything that is mixed together to make the dog food. Ingredients can be of nutritional or non-nutritional value. Fat, proteins, carbohydrates, vitamins, and minerals are nutritional components of dog food. Non-nutritional ingredients include food additives, artificial coloring, artificial flavorings, and food preservatives.

Dog food labels list ingredients in decreasing order of preponderance by weight. In other words, if the label lists beef, rice, and chicken as ingredients, this means there is more beef than rice or chicken in the mixture, and more rice than chicken in the mixture. However, it does not mean that there is more beef than rice and chicken combined. It also does not tell you how much more beef there is than chicken or rice or what percent of each ingredient makes up the total mixture. If beef is listed as the first ingredient, it is possible that there is only slightly more beef in the mixture than rice. Finally, it also does not tell you the quality or digestibility of the ingredients. For example, unless indicated, you do not know which beef parts make up the beef.

When you first bring your Pom puppy home, feed him the same food the breeder was feeding him. If a change in diet is necessary, make the change gradually to avoid stomach upset.

Different dog food manufacturers may use the same types of ingredients, but the ingredients may vary in quality. It is no wonder dog food labels can be confusing and misleading. You cannot rely strictly on the comparison of ingredient labels to determine which dog food is best for your Pom's needs.

Nutrients

Nutrients are necessary for life's processes. Some nutrients, such as sugars, amino acids (the building blocks of proteins), and fatty acids, produce energy. Other nutrients may not produce energy, but are required for life just the same. Among the more obvious life-supporting non-energy-producing nutrients are water, oxygen, vitamins, and minerals. The type and amount of nutrients contained in a dog food mixture make up the nutrient profile.

Nutritional Adequacy

The American Association of Feed Control Officials (AAFCO) requires dog food companies to demonstrate the nutritional adequacy of their products, either by feeding trials or by meeting the AAFCO Nutrient Profile. Feeding trials are the preferred method, but most companies simply calculate a formulation for a diet using a standard table of ingredients. Dog food companies are required to make a statement about the nutritional adequacy of all their products, except treats and snacks, such as "complete and balanced nutrition."

Proteins

The most important health factor in your Pom's diet is protein quality. To grow a beautiful coat, a Pomeranian needs high-quality protein. Research has shown that one-third of protein in canine diets is used for the support,

growth, and maintenance of skin and hair.

Proteins are not equal in nutritional value. High-quality animal-source proteins are better for dogs than plant-source proteins because they provide a better balance of amino acids and have a high biological value. Animal-source protein makes up the most expensive part of the diet. Do not confuse a high percentage of protein in the diet with high protein quality. There is a big difference. You can buy a dog food with a lot of protein, but if the high percentage of protein is poor-quality protein, your Pom will not be able to digest or use much of it.

If you are buying cheap dog food, it is unlikely that it contains high-quality protein.

Animal protein sources found in commercial dog foods include beef, chicken, turkey, duck, rabbit, lamb, venison, kangaroo, fish, and eggs. However, just because the protein comes from an animal source does not necessarily mean it is of high nutritional value.

Read the ingredients label closely and look for the words *meat, meal, and by-products*. Meat means muscle, skin, and organs composed of muscle (heart, diaphragm) and skin, with or without bone. By-products include heads, feet, guts, liver, kidneys, brain, spleen, and bone. By-products are less expensive and of poorer-quality protein. Meal tells you the protein source is ground up into particles (as in "cornmeal"). Meal may contain meat protein plus other tissues such as organs.

Meat protein may be higher-quality protein than plant protein sources, but Poms cannot live on meat alone. Like all canines, Pomeranians are carnivores (meat eaters), but this does not mean the diet must consist of 100 percent meat. In fact, an all-meat diet is not an adequate or complete diet for a Pomeranian—or any dog, for that matter. An all-meat diet is deficient in essential minerals (such as calcium) and other important components of the diet necessary for life.

Plant protein sources include soybean meal and soybean oil, and vegetables, such as corn. Corn is cheap, so it makes up a large component of many dog foods. Unfortunately, corn is fattening and also responsible for causing allergic skin conditions in many animals.

Poms can develop food allergies to various protein sources, especially beef and corn.

Fats

Fats are important components of your pet's daily diet. They add to the flavor of the food and influence skin and coat condition. Fats provide energy and play a major role in digestion and the assimilation of fat-soluble vitamins A, D, E, and K. The various fats (animal fat, vegetable oils, olive oil, fish oils) each have different effects on the body, and many are used for therapeutic remedies. Omega 3 and omega 6 fatty acids are important ingredients in your Pom's diet to promote healthy skin and coat.

Carbohydrates

Carbohydrates are sugars, starches, and fibers. They are an inexpensive source of energy compared with high-quality protein. *Researchers have not yet determined the exact amount of carbohydrates required in the canine diet, yet carbohydrates make up the major portion of today's commercial dog foods.* These carbohydrates usually are provided in the form of corn, cornmeal, rice, potatoes, wheat, or a combination of grains. Many dogs gradually develop an allergy to corn, corn meal, corn oil, or wheat and wheat gluten. These allergies often cause serious skin problems and can also cause gastrointestinal problems.

Because dogs cannot digest fiber, it is used in many dog foods to maintain dry matter bulk. Fiber, often supplied in the form of beet pulp, is used extensively in canine weight-reduction diets. Dogs on a high-fiber diet produce a lot more stool volume than dogs on a high-protein diet, because much of the food is not digested and is turned into waste matter. The more fiber in Max's diet, the greater the volume of excrement you will have to scoop. If you feed Max a highly digestible diet, most of the nutrition will be digested and used, and the amount of fecal output will be small.

If your Pom is overweight, consult your veterinarian about a reducing diet. The diet should be balanced to prevent hypoglycemia.

Vitamins

Depending on how vitamins are absorbed and excreted by the body, they are classified as fat-soluble (vitamins A, D, E, and K) or water-soluble (all the B vitamins and vitamin C). Dogs are capable of making their own vitamin C and do not require supplementation in their diet (unlike humans, nonhuman primates, guinea pigs, and some fruit bats, who develop scurvy and die without dietary vitamin C). Vitamin E plays an important role in skin and coat health.

Vitamins must be correctly balanced in your Pom's diet. An overdose of vitamins is just as dangerous as a vitamin deficiency. Excess vitamin intake, or a vitamin deficiency, can both cause serious medical problems.

Minerals

Minerals are necessary for skeletal growth and development and muscle and nerve function. Among the minerals required for life are calcium, phosphorus, sodium, potassium, magnesium, zinc, selenium, iron, manganese, copper, and iodine.

If you feed your Pom a balanced diet, he should not need supplements. Be sure to consult your veterinarian about your Pom's specific nutritional requirements.

Minerals should be provided in a balanced ratio. Excessive supplementation of minerals can lead to serious medical conditions.

Additives and Preservatives

Additives and preservatives are substances added to dog food to improve or enhance color, flavor, and texture, and to extend product shelf life. Additives, such as antioxidants, are added to dog food to help keep fat in the food from becoming rancid over time. Other additives are used to slow down bacterial and fungal growth.

Many Pomeranian breeders have noted an improvement in their dogs' health, reproduction, and skin and coat quality when they discontinued feeding dog foods containing ethoyxyquin, a preservative. These breeders prefer to feed brands that use vitamin E (tocopherols) and vitamin C as natural preservatives.

Chemicals

Many farm animals, especially chickens and cattle, are fed hormones and antibiotics. Grain crops are often sprayed with pesticides. The possible health risks associated with eating products treated with chemicals have long been a consumer concern. If the safety of these foods for humans is questionable, it is reasonable to assume that harmful chemicals could have an even greater effect on a Pomeranian because of its tiny size and increased sensitivities. Ask your veterinarian about dog food brands available in your area that manufacture food from "organically" produced meats and produce.

Supplements

If you feed your Pom a high-quality dog food, nutritional supplementation of vitamins and minerals is most likely unnecessary. In fact, by supplementing Max with other products, you may disrupt the nutritional balance you are striving to provide.

Hypoglycemia is one of the greatest health risks for Pomeranians and a leading cause of death in very young Poms. If you feed your pet the right food, and enough of it, he should not have any problems. Nevertheless, it is always a good idea to keep a form of sugar supplement on hand to prevent hypoglycemia in cases of emergency, sudden weakness, illness, or stress. Ask your veterinarian about emergency glucose supplementation in the form of a paste, such as Nutrical, when to use it, and how much to give.

Always consult your veterinarian about any form of supplementation before adding it to your Pomeranian's nutritional program.

Homemade Diets

Unless you are a canine nutritional specialist, do not try to formulate your dog's diet or cook his dinner at home. Canine nutrition is a complicated specialty, and homemade diets usually fall far short of meeting a dog's nutritional requirements.

Raw Diets

Do not feed your Pomeranian any raw foods, including meat, chicken, eggs, fish, or bones (raw or cooked). Your Pom can be poisoned by toxins from *Salmonella* and *E. coli* bacteria found in raw meat and bones. Because of their tiny size, Poms can be more sensitive to these toxins than other animals may be, even in very small amounts. In addition, raw diets are not balanced and are not nutritionally adequate for your Pom's needs. Do not take chances with your pet's health!

How Much to Feed

Nutritional needs vary according to the stage of development, activity level, and environmental conditions. The basic feeding guidelines provided

Ignore your Pom if he begs. Don't give in to begging eyes or your gourmand Pom may become rotund!

on dog food labels are painted with a broad brush, a one-size-fits-all for dogs, according to weight.

But Pomeranians are unique and do not fall into a set category. They have high caloric needs and a fast metabolism, so you will have to determine your pet's food requirements with the help of your veterinarian, rather than according to dog food labels. Just as you would not eat the same type and amount of food as your next door neighbor, no two dogs are alike in their feeding requirements, and certainly a Pomeranian cannot be compared with a larger breed, or even with other toy breeds. Max's energy requirements and caloric intake will vary from those of other dogs and throughout life.

The amount you feed Max also depends on the quality of the food you provide. If you feed a high-quality dog food that is easily digested, a smaller amount is needed than if you feed a mediocre diet filled with bulk and fiber material that cannot be digested.

The best way to know if Max is eating the proper amount is to check his overall physical condition. *You should be able to feel the ribs, but they should not feel bony and should have a nice layer of flesh over them. You should not be able to see the ribs.* To be certain Max is eating enough, *feel* him. Do not let his heavy coat fool you into thinking he is bigger than he really is.

When to Feed

Pomeranian puppies are active individuals that burn off calories quickly. Their initial growth phase is during the first six months of life, although technically they are still puppies until eight to twelve months of age, when the bone plates have closed and growth is complete. While Max is a very young puppy, he should be fed free choice (also called free feeding, or *ad libitum*), which means that food is available at all times and he can eat whenever he desires. Free feeding helps prevent hypoglycemia.

After Max is six months of age, free feeding may continue to work well if he is a nibbler and not a glutton. Free feeding is convenient, but you should always measure the food so you know how much is eaten daily. If you leave

Once-a-day feeding is never enough for a Pomeranian!

food out during the day, be sure to discard old or stale food and replenish the dish with fresh food.

If Max is a gourmand with a tendency to overeat, he will eventually exceed his ideal weight unless he is fed individual meals. Active Poms may require four or more meals a day.

Be sure to feed your Pom on a regular schedule to prevent hypoglycemia and gastric upset, and always check with your veterinarian to be certain the feeding schedules and amounts match your pet's specific needs.

Obesity

Obesity is a form of malnutrition in which there is a ratio of too much fat to lean body tissue. We usually think of malnutrition as being a shortage of food, resulting in a thin, starved individual. However, malnutrition means bad nutrition (from the French word *mal* for *bad*). Malnutrition refers to all aspects of unbalanced nutrition, whether it is too little or too much.

Overeating is the most common cause of obesity in dogs. Obesity in dogs has now reached epidemic proportions in the United States—more than 30 percent of the canine population is obese. Unfortunately, obesity is also a common problem in Pomeranians. Just like humans, many Poms overeat and do not get enough exercise. Obesity is a serious health problem that can lead to heart disease, breathing problems, heatstroke from overheating, skeletal and joint problems (such as arthritis), and metabolic diseases (such as diabetes). An obese Pom loses his beautiful, light, flowing gait and waddles when he walks. His ribs cannot be felt because they are covered with a layer of fat. Even worse, a plump Pom's quality of life and longevity are robbed from him with every labored beat of his heart.

The good news is that obesity can easily be prevented. The most effective way to prevent Max from becoming overweight is to measure and monitor his food intake, avoid overfeeding, and give him regular exercise.

If your Pom is overweight, do not put him on a crash diet and do not exercise him rigorously. Consult your veterinarian for a weight reduction plan and exercise program that are *safe* for him!

Weighing In

Weigh your Pom once a week, if possible, and not less than once a month. You can do this by holding Max and weighing both of you on a bathroom scale, then weighing yourself alone. Subtract your weight from the combined weight and the difference is Max's weight. Another option is to ask your veterinarian if you can use the hospital baby scale each week. If you notice any weight loss or gain, your veterinarian can advise you if Max is within the appropriate weight range and whether to change the diet or meal size. Remember that an adult Pomeranian weighs 3 to 7 pounds (1.36 to 3.18 kg), so do not let Max become too heavy or too thin.

Water

Water is the most important of all nutrients. Water is necessary for life because it is needed for digestion, to metabolize energy, and to eliminate waste products from the body. Although you would never deprive Max of food, he could survive longer without food than without water. A 10 percent body water loss can result in death, and water makes up more than 70 percent of your Pom's adult body weight.

Dogs lose body water throughout the day, in the urine and feces, and by evaporation, panting, drooling, and sweating through the foot pads. Water depletion occurs more rapidly in warm or hot weather or when an animal is

Make sure your Pom has fresh, clean water available at all times.

active. Body water must be replaced continually, so Max must have fresh water available at all times to avoid dehydration and illness. It is also very important that you not leave him outside in hot weather. Pomeranians are Nordic dogs that were originally acclimated to cold climates. They cannot tolerate hot weather.

Make sure Max drinks enough water every day. If he is continually thirsty or drinks more than usual, these could be warning signs of illness, such as diabetes or kidney (renal) disease. If he is not drinking as much as he should, he can become dehydrated and develop health problems. If you think Max is drinking too much, or not drinking enough, contact your veterinarian right away.

Food Myths

There are some common myths about the effects of various foods in the canine diet. Garlic is often credited with killing worms and repelling fleas. Brewer's yeast and onions also have been touted as flea repellents. Unfortunately, these foods have no action against internal or external parasites, although dogs can benefit from the B vitamins in brewer's yeast. Onions, on the other hand, can cause toxicity in dogs and are not recommended in the diet.

Food Allergies

Pomeranians can develop food allergies that cause itchy, reddened skin and hair loss. In severe cases hair loss and sore spots can extend to the feet, legs, face, and ears. More than half the cases of hair loss around the head and neck in Pomeranians are caused by food allergies.

If Max is scratching his skin excessively for no apparent reason, and his coat does not look its best, ask your veterinarian if a hypoallergenic diet would be beneficial. Hypoallergenic diets are developed especially for dogs with skin sensitivities and food allergies. They may contain ingredients such as fish, duck, venison, egg, potato, or rice. They do not contain beef, corn, or other foods known to cause skin problems in dogs.

Good Eating Habits

• Do not allow your Pomeranian to beg.
• Free-feed or feed on a regular schedule.
• Feed enough to satisfy your pet's nutritional needs.
• Do not feed food intended for humans, especially snack foods and candies. The high sugar and salt content in junk "people food" is as bad for dogs as it is for humans.
• Do not feed bones. They can splinter and become lodged in the throat or gastrointestinal tract.
• Feed healthful snacks and treats primarily as training rewards or special praise.
• Teach children not to feed meals or give treats to your Pom without your permission.

Chapter Nine

Keeping Your Pomeranian Healthy

Pomeranians are sturdy little dogs that can live up to fifteen years or longer, so Pomeranian ownership is definitely a long-term commitment. A big part of that commitment, and the key to your Pom's longevity, is giving her the best care you possibly can. If Charm is healthy, she is more likely to live a longer, happier life. That means more years for you to spend together!

Preventive Health Care

There is no better gift that you can give your Pomeranian than the gift of good health care. You can do a lot to keep her as healthy as possible throughout her life. It is quick and easy to take a few moments every day to check her thoroughly while you play with her. Check her eyes, ears, nose, mouth, skin, feet, and area under the tail. Take note of her basic behaviors: eating, drinking, urinating, defecating, activity level, attitude, walking, running, playfulness. Your observations can make all the difference between finding a problem in its early stage and treating it immediately and successfully, or finding a problem too late, when it has become serious.

Your pampered Pom is a lucky pup! First, she is a member of a strong, hardy breed and is not affected by many health problems, especially when compared with other toy breeds. Second, she lives during a time when most canine health problems and diseases can be prevented or treated—problems that, through the ages and until relatively recently, killed dogs by the hundreds of thousands. Malnutrition, severe parasitism, and bacterial and viral diseases were among the top canine killers. Today's Pomeranian owners are more educated and conscientious about their precious Poms than ever before, and as a result, their little companions are enjoying better health and living longer. When help or guidance is needed for additional quality care, veterinarians, including certified specialists, are there to assist with the latest in medical advances, technology, and prescription products.

Pomeranians also benefit greatly from today's superior nutrition offered in specially formulated and balanced diets. And, because Pomeranians are house dogs and family members, they

With good care, Pomeranians can live fifteen years or more.

Preventive health care is the most important care you can give your Pomeranian.

love to share all the creature comforts that people enjoy.

It is reassuring to know that countless resources are available if needed, but the best way to keep your Pomeranian healthy is to *prevent* problems.

Preventive health care includes regular physical examinations, vaccinations against disease, an effective parasite control program, balanced nutrition appropriate for your Pom's life stage, regular skin and coat care and grooming, and daily exercise. Pomeranians are not sedentary lap

dogs. They are animated and energetic. They need to keep busy and they need daily exercise.

Good dental care is very important for all Pomeranians. Plaque accumulation, periodontal disease, and other dental problems, such as retained baby teeth, are common in Poms.

Of course, all Poms need plenty of love and attention for their physical and mental well-being. Pomeranians are smart, affectionate, charismatic, people-pleasing dogs that deserve the very best of care and a lot of love!

Selecting a Veterinarian

Choosing the right veterinarian for Charm is a very important first step in her health care. Find a veterinarian who is familiar with Pomeranians—one who recognizes and understands their special breed characteristics and conditions and who appreciates Pomeranians as much as you do.

It is best to look for a veterinarian *before* you need one, so that you are not burdened with such an important decision during an emergency situation. Be just as selective in choosing Charm's doctor as you are about choosing your own physician.

Here are some guidelines to help you select the right veterinarian.

1. Reputation: Ask Charm's breeder, other Pomeranian owners, dog trainers, dog groomers, and members of your local kennel club which veterinarians they recommend.

Word of mouth is one of the best ways to find a veterinarian.

2. Visit: A visit to the veterinary clinic will help you in the decision-making process. Ask for an appointment to meet the doctors and staff and tour the veterinary hospital facility that you are considering. Pay special attention to cleanliness and odors. Ask about the availability of special equipment for surgery and anesthesia of toy breeds.

3. Training: The veterinary support staff will play an important role in Charm's health care, so do not be shy about inquiring about the training and experience of the veterinary nurses. Ask if the nurses are licensed registered veterinary technicians and how long they have worked at the practice. A long-term staff is a good sign of a stable, dedicated practice.

4. Location: When possible, find a veterinary hospital near you, preferably one that offers twenty-four-hour emergency service, so that in case of emergency you do not lose precious time and can reach the hospital quickly.

5. Convenience: Find a veterinary practice that offers services during hours that are convenient for you, including one that offers extended or weekend hours.

6. Continuity: Whenever possible, it is best if the same doctor(s) see Charm on a regular basis so nothing is overlooked and her case is known

Take your Pom pup to your veterinarian right away to make sure she is healthy and to set up a regular health care program.

Health Insurance for Dogs

Several companies offer health insurance for dogs. If Charm is registered with the American Kennel Club, you can enroll her in the AKC health insurance program. Your veterinarian can recommend a pet health care insurance policy that is right for your Pom.

in detail and followed closely. When there is a lack of continuity, there can be a lack of communication. Something could be overlooked in Charm's medical record.

7. Communication: List your questions and concerns for the doctor so that you make the most of Charm's appointment and do not forget important questions.

8. Emergency clinics: If your veterinarian does not offer emergency care, or all-night/holiday/weekend care for serious illness or injury, then

you must also select an emergency hospital near you. Visit the emergency hospitals to decide which to use as backup in case Charm needs urgent care and hospitalization. Emergency situations are very stressful. They often occur at night or on holidays, when everyone is tired. Make a practice drive to the emergency hospital—and hope that you never have to make the drive for a real reason! This way you know in advance the best route to take to get there quickly and will not be distracted by directions and maps in an emergency situation.

9. Fees: Ask about fees for the type of services Charm may need. Veterinarians give price estimates for anticipated services, and most expect payment when service is rendered, unless payment arrangements have been made in advance. Ask what types of payment methods are available.

The Home Health Check

It is easy to tell when a Pomeranian is feeling great. Poms are alert, active, inquisitive, underfoot, or at your side. Anything less than an animated, bright-eyed, busybody means that your Pom may have a problem. If Charm is not acting like herself, seems depressed, does not want to eat, is lethargic, is losing weight, or has any other problems, call your veterinarian right away to make an appointment for a physical examination and diagnosis. The sooner you recognize a problem, the better you can help Charm.

A home health check is a good way to detect possible problems early. A home checkup is not a replacement for the veterinary examination, but it gives you a good idea of your Pom's health condition. Keep a record of Charm's condition, noting dates and times. This information will be useful in assessing the progression or improvement of a condition over time.

To identify subtle signs of illness in a Pomeranian, you must first be able to recognize normal appearance, attitude, stance, movement, and behavior. Here are things to look for, from the nose to the toes, when you examine your Pomeranian.

1. Overall picture: Your Pom should be outgoing, alert, happy, bold, and in overall good condition, with a healthy, beautiful coat. She should be well proportioned, not too thin and not too heavy. Use your hands to feel through the profuse coat. *You should be able to feel the ribs slightly, but not see them.* However, with all that hair, you would not see the ribs even if Charm was very thin, so you must feel to be sure. Charm should not feel bony or skinny.

2. Natural stance: Observe Charm while she stands. She should stand naturally and place her weight on all four feet equally, without favoring a foot. A hunched-up posture can mean back or abdominal pain. A drooping head may indicate neck, chest, or front limb pain. A tilted head could be caused by ear pain, ear infection, parasites in the ear, or a nervous system problem.

3. Movement (gait): Charm should walk, trot, and run willingly and normally, without difficulty or limping. Pomeranian gait can be hard to assess because Pomeranians are small, have lots of hair, and move very quickly. Any "skipping" or "hopping" is often a sign of a luxated patella (slipped kneecap), a common problem in toy breeds, including Pomeranians. One way to better evaluate your pet's gait is to videotape her and then play the videotape back in slow motion.

4. Legs and feet: Charm's feet and legs should be pain-free. When you feel the hind limbs, pay special attention to whether any bones feel like they slip or pop. These are often signs of patellar luxation. Sometimes lameness is difficult to detect, especially if there is lameness in more than one limb. Lameness can be caused by injury, bone and joint problems, muscular problems, nervous system problems, a cut foot pad, or a foreign object. Pomeranians have a lot of hair between the toes, so thorns, stickers, and grass awns may be hidden and hard to see. They can cause pain and infection, so check all four of Charm's feet and between the toes after every outing. Check the nail beds for redness and infection. Check for torn toenails. Pay attention to the dewclaws (the innermost small toenails). These should be trimmed regularly or they can curl and grow into the tissues of the leg, causing pain and infection.

5. Face: A cold, wet nose is normal, although a dry nose does not mean illness. Charm's nose should be free of discharge, thick mucus, or pus. If Charm plays and digs outside, she may have dirt lodged in the little cor-

If your Pom pup does not look healthy, or acts like she is depressed or not feeling well, call your veterinarian immediately.

ner grooves of her nose (the nares). Clear dirt away gently from her small nostrils with a soft, damp tissue.

6. Eyes: *All eye problems require immediate veterinary attention. Many eye problems are painful. Some eye problems may appear minor but can result in loss of sight or loss of the eye.* Eyes should be bright and clear. If any mucus has accumulated around the eyes, gently remove it with a tissue. If you observe squinting, redness, irritation, excess mucus, or infection (green or yellow discharge) in or around the eyes, or if the colored part of the eye (the iris) or the surface of the eye appear cloudy or hazy, contact your veterinarian immediately. Pomeranians may develop cataracts or corneal

The Basics: Vital Signs

- Heart rate: You can take your Pomeranian's heart rate in two ways:

1. Place your fingers between your dog's ribs on the left side of the chest, behind the elbow and feel the heartbeat.

2. Place your fingers on the inside middle portion of either upper thigh. You can also place your finger in the groin area where the leg connects to the body. Count the number of pulses you feel in a minute. *Normal resting pulse is 80 to 180 beats per minute, depending on whether your Pom is at rest or has just been very active.*

- Temperature: Take your Pom's temperature rectally. A digital thermometer is recommended. Lubricate the tip of the rectal thermometer and gently insert it a distance of about 1 inch (2.5 cm) into your pet's rectum. Support your dog so she does not sit on the thermometer, and try to keep her calm.

Normal Pomeranian body temperature ranges from 100 to 102°F (38–39°C). A very excited Pom may have an elevated temperature as high as 102.5°F (39.5°C), but it should not exceed this value.

- Circulation: Capillary refill time (CRT) is a good indicator of circulation. Press on the gums for a second with your finger. The gums should return to a bright pink color as the capillaries refill. *Normal CRT is two seconds or less.*
- Respiration rate: Count how many breaths your Pom takes in one minute. Respiration rate increases with excitement, heat, or difficulty breathing.

Normal respiration is fifteen to thirty breaths per minute.

- Hydration: Lift the skin over the shoulders and let go. The skin should quickly fall back over the shoulders. If the skin is slow to drop, or remains "tented," then your Pom is dehydrated and needs fluids.

edema. In both cases the eyes will appear cloudy. Poms can also suffer from entropion, a rolling inward of the eyelids so that the lids and lashes rub on the surface of the eye. Pay close attention to whether Charm appears to see well. Pomeranians can inherit progressive retinal atrophy (PRA), an incurable hereditary disease that eventually leads to blindness.

7. Mouth: *Bad breath is not normal in dogs and is an indicator of health problems, such as periodontal disease.* More than 85 percent of adult Pomeranians suffer from some degree of periodontal disease unless they routinely have their teeth cleaned and polished. If Charm has bad breath, she probably has dental problems. However, depending on the odor, some types of bad breath indicate a metabolic problem. Gums should be bright pink and teeth should be free of tartar accumulation. Dental problems, including retained deciduous (baby) teeth, are common in Pomeranians.

Check your Pom's coat thoroughly for stickers, burrs, grass awns, mats, ticks, and fleas every time she plays outdoors.

8. Ears: Check the ears for dirt and wax buildup. Pomeranian ears need regular cleaning. Hair can accumulate near the ear canal and create a moist, warm environment ideal for bacterial and fungal growth. If Charm's ears are sensitive, painful, reddened, or have a foul odor, or if she shakes her head and scratches at her ears, contact your veterinarian right away for medical care. Charm could have a bacterial or fungal ear infection, parasites (such as mites or fleas), or foreign objects (such as a grass awn or "foxtail") in her ears.

9. Skin and hair: Part the thick coat in many areas all over Charm's body to make sure the skin is healthy. It should not be dry, flaky, or greasy, and it should be free of parasites, such as fleas, ticks, lice, and mange mites. Pomeranians are predisposed to some hair loss and skin conditions, such as hyposomatotropism alopecia

X, "hair cycle arrest." If Charm starts to shed excessively or her skin does not look healthy, consult your veterinarian.

10. Sexual maturity: Check Charm regularly for signs of estrus if she has not yet been spayed. If you have an intact male, both of his testicles should be fully descended into the scrotum. If one or both testicles are missing, contact your veterinarian. Retained testicles are not uncommon in Pomeranians and may be an inherited problem. If the retained testicle is not surgically removed, it can develop cancer in later life.

11. The "south end": Check underneath the tail for problems such as swelling, hernias, anal sac impaction (not unusual in Pomeranians) or abscesses, cysts, inflammation, diarrhea, and parasites (tapeworms). Prevent fecal material from becoming matted on the hair under the tail. This

Core vaccines (recommended)	Noncore vaccines (optional)	Not recommended
Canine parvovirus (MLV*)	Parainfluenza	Canine coronavirus
Canine distemper (MLV)	Bordetella	Giardia lambia
Canine adenovirus-2 (MLV)	Borrelia burgdorferi	
(Hepatitis)	(Lyme disease)	
Rabies (killed virus)	Leptospira	

*MLV: Modified live virus vaccine

attracts flies, especially in the summer. If your Pom is dirty under the tail, flies can land and lay hundreds of eggs in the matted material. Maggot infestation results quickly, and while hidden in the matted feces and hair, can go unnoticed while fly larvae invade, infect, and destroy the animal's body tissues in a very short time.

Vaccinations

Vaccinations (inoculations, immunizations) are the best method available to protect Charm against serious, life-threatening diseases. Although you do your best to prevent her from coming into contact with sick animals, at some time your Pom will be exposed to germs that cause illness. Anywhere you take her—parks, beaches, rest stops, campgrounds, dog shows, obedience classes, even your veterinarian's office—Charm can be exposed to viruses, bacteria, and protozoa that can cause severe diseases and even death. Although there is not a vaccine available for every known canine disease, we do have vaccines for the most common and deadly diseases.

No vaccine is 100 percent guaranteed effective. However, if you are diligent about Charm's health and vaccination schedule, she has a very good chance of being protected against serious contagious diseases.

Your veterinarian will make vaccine recommendations—which immunizations to give and what schedule to follow—specific to your Pom's needs. For example, most Pomeranians are house dogs that are unlikely to be in areas where they can contract Leptospirosis or Lyme disease. Therefore, vaccinations for these diseases are not routinely recommended for Pomeranians. If, however, your Pom will be going camping with you or taking a wilderness hike, your veterinarian may make special recommendations.

Pomeranian puppies are tiny and sensitive. Your veterinarian may separate the time interval between vaccines by a few days or a week or more, rather than giving them all at one time. For example, your veterinarian may give Charm her distemper and hepatitis vaccines on one visit and her rabies vaccine one month later. By spacing some of the vaccinations, your pet's immune system may

No two Poms are alike. Vaccine schedules and the vaccines to be given should be determined according to your Pom's age, health, and risk of disease exposure.

Guideline Schedule for Core Vaccines for Pomeranian Puppies

Vaccine	First inoculation	Second inoculation	Third inoculation	First booster	Follow-up
	Age	Age	Age	Interval	Interval
Distemper	8 weeks	12 weeks	16 weeks	1 year	Every 3 years
Canine adenovirus-2 Hepatitis	8 weeks	12 weeks	16 weeks	1 year	Every 3 years
Parvovirus*	8 weeks	12 weeks	16 weeks	1 year	Every 3 years
Rabies	12 weeks to 16 weeks (state laws vary)			1 year	Every 3 years

*Some veterinarians recommend a fourth parvovirus vaccination at twenty weeks of age because many dogs do not develop sufficient immunity against this disease before they are five months of age.

Common Canine Diseases That Can Be Prevented by Immunizations

Disease	Cause	Spread
Distemper	Viral	Airborne, body excretions
Parvovirus	Viral	Contaminated feces
Infectious canine hepatitis	Viral	Body excretions, urine
Leptospirosis	Bacterial	Urine contaminated in kennels or from wild animals
Parainfluenza Bordetellosis Both cause "kennel cough."	Viral Bacterial	Airborne, sneeze and cough droplets
Lyme disease	Bacterial	Spread by the bite of an infected tick or contaminated body fluids
Rabies	Viral	Saliva (bite wounds)
Rattlesnake bite	Rattlesnake venom	Rattlesnake bite wound

respond better to the vaccines and the chances of adverse vaccine reactions may be reduced.

The 2006 American Animal Hospital Association (AAHA) Canine Vaccine Guidelines updated recommendations divide vaccines into three categories:

1. Core vaccines: recommended

2. Noncore vaccines: optional, depending on the dog's risk of exposure

3. Not recommended

Vaccination is a medical decision, not a calendar event. The type of vaccination, and when it is given, should be determined according to your

Contagion	Signs
Highly contagious, especially among young dogs	Difficulty breathing, coughing, discharge from nose and eyes, vomiting, diarrhea, dehydration, trembling, blindness, paralysis, seizures, skin pustules, hard foot pads
Highly contagious, especially among puppies	Diarrhea, dehydration, vomiting, heart problems, and heart failure
Highly contagious, especially among puppies and young dogs	Liver inflammation, jaundice, "blue eye" caused by inflammation and fluid buildup, kidney damage, pain, and internal bleeding
Highly contagious	Kidney and liver damage, jaundice, kidney failure, internal bleeding, anemia
Highly contagious, especially in boarding kennels	Dry, hacking, continual cough of several weeks duration that may cause permanent damage to airways
	Swollen lymph nodes, lethargy, loss of appetite, joint swelling, lameness, heart and kidney disease
	Fatal, preceded by nervous system signs, including paralysis, incoordination, and change in behavior
Not contagious	Pain, swelling, weakness, tissue damage, shock, death

Pom's lifestyle, age, health condition, past medical history, and potential risk of exposure. There are significant benefits, as well as some risks, associated with any vaccine.

The vaccination schedule on page 111 should be considered only as a guideline.

Adult booster vaccinations should be given as recommended by your veterinarian based on your Pomeranian's health and specific requirements.

Treatments

• Viral infections: There is no treatment to kill the virus once infection

Internal Parasites

	Transmission to dogs
Roundworms	Ingestion of eggs in feces of infected animals, transmitted from mother to pup *in utero* or in the milk
Hookworms	Ingestion of larvae in feces of infected animals, direct skin contact with larvae
Whipworms	Contact with feces
Tapeworms	Contact with fleas and feces, ingestion of fleas, eating raw meat (wild rodents)
Heartworms	Mosquito bite
Protozoa	Contact with feces

Flea control is a very important part of health care. Fleas are external parasites that cause skin problems and allergies. Heavily infested Poms can suffer from anemia (low number of red blood cells) and die because of the large amount of blood fleas take from them. Fleas also spread tapeworms which are intestinal parasites that rob the animal of nutrients.

has occurred. Treatment consists of supportive therapy such as fluids, antibiotics to control secondary bacterial infection, medications, and rest.

• Rabies virus: *Post*-exposure treatment exists for humans but not for animals.

• Bacterial infections: Antibiotics and supportive therapy are necessary.

• Rattlesnake bites: Rattlesnake antivenin is available.

Parasite Control

Parasite control is easy. It is hard to believe that not so long ago severe parasite infestation was a common cause of death in dogs, especially young puppies. Fortunately, today we have a wide selection of effective parasiticides (products that kill parasites). Internal parasites (roundworms, hookworms, whipworms, tapeworms, and heartworms) and external parasites (fleas, ticks, ear mites, lice, and

Transmission to humans	Prevention
Accidental ingestion of eggs from contact with infected fecal material	Some parasiticides may be given to very young pups. Dewormings should be repeated as necessary.
Direct skin contact with larvae in soil contaminated with feces of infected animals, accidental ingestion of larvae	Parasiticides
No	Parasiticides
Accidental ingestion	Parasiticides
No	Parasiticides
Accidental ingestion of organisms in fecal material	Parasiticides

mange-causing mites) can be killed and controlled with medications available as once-a-month tablets, topical applications, or by injection.

Even though Charm lives indoors with you, she can "acquire" several kinds of external parasites on her daily outings. Be on the lookout, especially during summer months, for fleas and ticks. Your Pom's profuse coat is a skin parasite's paradise! The number one cause of scratching and hair loss in dogs is flea infestation. After every outing check Charm's skin and hair closely and take time to brush out her coat.

Internal Parasites

Internal parasites, such as worms and protozoa, can have a serious effect on your Pomeranian's health. Because Poms are so small, they cannot tolerate parasite infestations as well as some larger breeds, and can rapidly deteriorate from the diar-

Check your Pom's skin regularly for parasites, sores, rashes, and foreign bodies. Lay her on her side and thoroughly check the belly, groin, chest, and axillary (armpit) areas.

External Parasites

	Animal health problem	Contagious to humans
Fleas	Allergy to flea saliva, skin irritation and itching, hair loss, transmission of tapeworms	Fleas may bite humans. Tapeworms also may be indirectly transmitted to people.
Ticks	Transmission of Lyme disease, skin irritation and infection	Humans can contract Lyme disease from direct contact with ticks. Always wear gloves when removing ticks from your dog to avoid contracting the disease.
Sarcoptic mange	Skin lesions and itching, hair loss	Sarcoptic mange can spread from pets to people by contact.
Demodectic mange	Skin lesions, localized or generalized hair loss	No

rhea, dehydration, anemia, irritation, and malnutrition parasites cause.

Be sure to have Charm checked for internal parasites. Fecal examinations are required to look for tiny parasite eggs and organisms under the microscope. Tapeworms are large enough to see in the feces or around the anal area. They are flat and resemble

grains of rice or cucumber seeds and may be alive and moving, or dried up and dead. A few drops of blood are needed to test for heartworm.

Many internal parasites of dogs, such as roundworms, tapeworms, hookworms, and protozoa (*Giardia lambia*) are transmitted through contact with feces and can pose a health threat to people, especially children. Prevention is simple: good hygiene, a clean environment, and teaching children to wash their hands after handling animals and before eating.

Illness

Pomeranians are small, and when illness strikes, it can hit hard. If Charm

From the nose to the toes, your veterinarian will do a complete physical examination to make sure your Pom is in excellent health.

is not acting like herself, there is a reason. Play it safe. Take her to your veterinarian right away at the first signs of anything unusual. Lack of appetite, lethargy, inactivity, or depression should be taken very seriously. Pomeranians are bright, playful, active dogs, and changes in behavior indicate a problem. Early treatment makes all the difference between rapid recovery and prolonged illness, or even death.

Contact your veterinarian if your Pom has any of the following problems:

Fever
Pain
Loss of appetite
Lethargy
Vomiting
Diarrhea
Constipation
Discharge from the eyes
Breathing problems
Coughing, sneezing, wheezing
Choking
Lameness
Head shaking
Trembling
Blood in the urine or stools
Inability to urinate or defecate
Seizures
Dehydration
Weight loss

First Aid for Your Pomeranian

In spite of all your efforts to provide a safe environment for your Pomeranian, accidents can happen, and many are

Do not use Kaopectate or Pepto-bismol for treatment of gastric upset or diarrhea. These products used to be safe for pets; however, their formulations have changed and they are no longer recommended for animal use. Ask your veterinarian for a suitable replacement.

life threatening. *The difference between life and death for your Pomeranian could depend on how prepared you are in an emergency situation.*

Prepare an emergency kit right now! Put all your supplies together *today* so you do not waste precious time during an emergency trying to find what you need. Write down the doses for different medications and put the list in the kit. That way you can give the medicine without having to figure out the dose in the middle of a crisis. Make a copy of the emergency instructions in this book and put it in your first aid kit so you can refer to it easily. Keep your veterinarian's daytime and emergency telephone numbers near the phone and keep an additional copy in the first aid kit, along with the phone number for the poison control center. Put the first aid kit in a special place.

When you travel with Charm, take her first aid kit with you. You may want to include additional items for the trip, such as bottled water, a balanced electrolyte solution (such as Pedialyte), medication to prevent carsickness, tranquilizers, and pain killers.

Supplies for Your Pom's First Aid Kit

The basic supplies and materials you need for your first aid kit can be purchased at your local pharmacy or from your veterinarian.

First aid kit supplies:

- Bandage scissors
- Small, regular, blunt-tipped scissors
- Thermometer
- Tourniquet (a strip of gauze will work)
- Tweezers
- Forceps
- Mouth gag (small wooden dowel will work)
- Hydrogen peroxide 3 percent solution
- Triple antibiotic ointment

Protect Your Pom, Protect Yourself: Use a Muzzle!

If you have not yet purchased a nylon muzzle, you can make a muzzle from a strip of gauze about 18 inches (46 cm) long. Wrap the gauze around your Pom's muzzle, as close to the face as possible, and tie it securely under the chin. Take the ends of the gauze and tie them behind the head. Do not let your Pom remove the muzzle with her front paws!

- Roll of gauze bandage
- Gauze pads
- Telfa no-stick pads
- Sterile dressing and compresses
- Sterile saline solution
- Elastic bandage (preferably waterproof)
- Self-adhesive bandage (Vet Wrap type)
- Activated charcoal (for treatment of poisoning)
- Eyewash
- Antihistamines (diphenhydramine or chlorpheneramine)
- Ophthalmic ointment (should *not* contain hydrocortisone)
- Cold compress (instant cold type)
- Small muzzle (Buy a comfortable nylon muzzle. If you do not have a muzzle, a gauze strip will work.)
- Blanket
- Paper towels
- Soap (Novalsan or Hibiclens)
- Sponge
- Exam gloves (vinyl)
- Penlight
- Flashlight
- Bottled water
- Electrolyte solution, such as Pedialyte
- Nutrical or other high-sugar product such as corn syrup (Karo syrup)
- Plastic bags
- Clippers (optional, but handy to shave wound areas)
- Syringes (to give medicines and liquids)

First Aid Emergency Care

First aid means giving your Pom the emergency care she needs until veterinary help is available. Your first goal is to save Charm's life. Your sec-

If you take your Pom hiking or camping, watch for snakes and scorpions and remember to carry first aid treatment for insect stings.

ond goal is to reduce pain and suffering. Before starting any first aid treatment, the most important thing to do is protect yourself from being bitten or injured. Loving Poms can behave unpredictably when they are in pain or frightened. Charm may not recognize you or may snap at anyone who approaches. If someone else is available, save time by having that person contact your veterinarian for advice while you begin emergency treatment. You may need help restraining Charm while you treat her. The person who assists you should be experienced in small animal handling. Your Pom is small, but she is strong. She may struggle, and if she is not restrained correctly, she can be hurt.

Always muzzle your Pomeranian before initiating emergency treatment, for the safety of your pet and everyone involved.

Pomeranian ABCs: Airway, Breathing, Circulation

The most important things to check first in an emergency are the following:

1. Is the airway (trachea) unobstructed and open?
2. Is your Pom breathing?
3. Is the heart beating?

For all medical conditions and emergencies, contact your veterinarian immediately.

The friendship you share with your Pom will last for many years. Take excellent care of your little canine companion. She deserves it!

Airway

Pomeranians are very small and so are their parts. Charm has a tiny throat and even tinier trachea (windpipe). Carefully open her mouth wide to check if anything is blocking the air passageway. Poms have delicate jaws, so be gentle. Use a pen light to look down the throat to make sure the trachea is not obstructed with a foreign object (such as food, toy particles, or pebbles). If anything is blocking the air passage, remove it immediately to prevent suffocation. Do not push the object farther down the throat with your fingers. Forceps may be necessary to retrieve the object.

Breathing

If your Pom is not breathing, you must act quickly and breathe for her.

Open her mouth, remove any objects or debris, and clear away secretions. Place your mouth over Charm's nose and muzzle so that it makes a tight seal. Breathe into her nostrils gently and watch for her chest to rise. Release so air can be expelled. Repeat this procedure every five seconds until your Pom breathes on her own. Blow gently, but enough to make the chest rise. Blowing too hard can damage your dog's tiny lungs. Check gum color periodically. The gums should return to a bright pink color if Charm is receiving enough oxygen.

Note: Be careful! It is safest to do this procedure only if your Pom is unconscious, or you may be bitten!

Cardiac

If you cannot hear a heartbeat or feel a pulse, begin cardiopulmonary resuscitation (CPR) immediately so blood can circulate and bring oxygen to the lungs. Place your pet on her right side. Place both hands on top of each other and gently press your fingers on the left side of Charm's chest, slightly above and directly behind the elbow. Continue to press and release at a rate of one to two presses every second. Remember to also breathe into the nostrils every ten seconds. Continue CPR until your pet is able to breathe on her own and you can feel a pulse.

Bite Wounds

The most common wounds Poms suffer are bite wounds, usually from being attacked by larger dogs. Because of their small size, protective nature, and bold personality, Pomeranians seldom back off from aggressors. Wounds to the head, neck, chest, and abdomen can be very serious. Wounds that penetrate the body cavity are life threatening, especially if the lungs are partially collapsed or the internal organs are exposed. Immediate emergency veterinary care is needed.

If your Pom has an abdominal wound in which the body organs are protruding, cover them gently with a warm, sterile, damp saline dressing. Do not push the organs back into the body. Rush your Pom to the hospital.

Bite wounds require thorough cleansing and antibiotics to prevent infection. If the wound is a laceration or tear, it may need to be sutured. Puncture wounds should be cleaned well with a disinfectant solution, and most are allowed to remain open to drain. Look carefully through your Pom's thick, profuse coat. It is easy to miss a serious bite wound or injury under all the hair.

Contact your veterinarian immediately about any bite wound injuries. In the unlikely event that a stray or wild animal has bitten Charm, discuss the possible risk of rabies with your veterinarian.

Bleeding

Bleeding or hemorrhage occurs from injury, trauma, or serious health problems. Use a gauze or clean towel as a compress to apply firm pressure over the wound to stop the bleeding. If a large blood vessel in a limb has been severed, hemorrhage is life-threatening, and you cannot stop the bleeding, apply a tourniquet above the cut area. Be sure to loosen the tourniquet every ten minutes to relieve pressure and allow circulation. Contact your veterinarian immediately. What may seem to be a small amount of blood loss can actually be a lot for a Pomeranian.

Bone Fractures

Poms have small skeletons and delicate bones that break easily, so it is not surprising that fractures are among the most common injuries Pomeranians suffer. Many fractures are caused by owners accidentally stepping on their Poms as they run about underfoot. Other Pom fractures are caused by being dropped by children, falling off of furniture, or being roughed up by large dogs.

Signs of bone fractures include swelling, pain and tenderness, abnormal limb position or movement, limping, and crepitation (a crackling sensation when the area is touched). When bones are broken, they may remain under the skin or protrude up through it (open fracture). If the bone is exposed, do not try to replace it or cleanse it. Stop the bleeding and cover the wound with a sterile bandage. Do not allow Charm to lick and contaminate the open fracture.

Because Pomeranians are so small, it is difficult to make proper splints for them. This is a job for your veterinarian. Instead, make your pet as comfortable as you can, place her on a soft bed, keep her calm, quiet, and warm, and restrict her activity. The best thing you can do is get Charm to your veterinarian as soon as possible.

Burns

Your Pomeranian can suffer three kinds of burns:

Thermal burns—from fire, boiling liquids, appliances

Electrical burns—from chewing on electrical cords

Chemical burns—from a variety of chemicals (such as corrosives, oxidizing agents, desiccants, and poisons)

If Charm is burned, immediately cool the burn by applying a cold, wet cloth or an ice pack to the area. Protect the burned area from the air with an ointment (Neosporin or Aloe vera). If she has suffered a chemical burn, immediately flush the burn profusely with water or saline to dilute and rinse the caustic chemical from the area.

Do not allow Charm to lick the area or she will burn her mouth and esophagus with the substance. Contact your veterinarian immediately.

Choking

Choking occurs when an object (such as bones, food, toys, or pebbles) becomes trapped, or lodged, in the mouth or throat, or accidentally inhaled into the trachea (windpipe). When an object obstructs the air passageway completely, the animal dies of suffocation.

If Charm is choking, try to get a good, clear view of her mouth and throat to see if the object can be safely removed. Pomeranians have very small jaws and it is difficult to look into the mouth. A short wooden dowel—2–3 inches (5–6 cm) in diameter—inserted between the back molars, may serve as a gag to hold the mouth open while you use a flashlight to take a closer look down the throat. If you see the foreign object, be very careful not to push it farther down the throat or into the trachea. Remove the object with forceps when possible, to avoid being bitten.

Cuts

Cuts should be cleansed well and treated with antibiotics to prevent infection. Serious cuts may require sutures, so contact your veterinarian for advice. If the cut is not too deep, clip the hair around it, wash it with a mild soap, and rinse it several times with water. Clean the injury with a disinfectant solution. Dry the wound well and apply an antibiotic ointment to it. Keep the wound clean and dry until it heals. If the cut is in an area that can be bandaged, wrap the area with gauze and bandage to prevent contamination and infection. *Change the bandage daily.*

Dehydration

Dehydration means the body has lost too much water. The most common causes of dehydration in Pomeranians are vomiting, diarrhea, and exposure to excessive heat. A dehydrated Pom has also lost important minerals from the body.

Treatment for dehydration is the replenishment of fluids. If Charm is conscious, offer her water to drink. Do

Poms can suffer from heat stroke, dehydration, and low blood sugar. Make sure your Pom has enough to eat, is protected from hot weather, and has lots of fresh water available at all times.

Do not give your Pomeranian homemade salt or sugar mixtures without first consulting your veterinarian. In the wrong proportions, these will do more harm than good and further dehydrate your dog.

not force water down her throat if she is unconscious or too weak to drink on her own. Doing so may cause her to aspirate water into her lungs. Keep a bottle of Pedialyte on hand for emergencies. Contact your veterinarian immediately.

Dystocia

Dystocia is the term used when a pregnant female has difficulty giving birth to her young. Dystocia is a common problem in Pomeranians. It occurs when the smooth muscles of the uterus become fatigued and weakened and can no longer contract. Dystocia also occurs when the uterus becomes twisted, or when the mother's pelvic area is abnormal or too small to allow passage of the puppy. In some cases, dystocia is caused by a puppy that is too large or is not in an appropriate birth position.

(It is normal for puppies to be born either rear feet first, or head first.)

Pomeranians average two to three puppies in a litter, although litter size can be larger. Even though Pomeranian puppies are very small, their rounded heads are large compared with the size of the mother's birth canal. Surgical intervention (cesarean section, also called a C-section) is often necessary to save the fragile, tiny pups.

If Charm is pregnant, give your veterinarian advance notice of her delivery due date and make backup arrangements for emergency care in case your veterinarian is unavailable the day she is due to whelp (give birth).

Never leave a Pomeranian in hard labor for more than one hour. A Pomeranian that has not whelped a pup within that time period, or that has stopped labor altogether, needs immediate veterinary care.

Heatstroke

Heatstroke is caused by exposure to high temperature and stress. Poms are heavy coated Nordic dogs of Spitz ancestry that originated from a very cold region. As such, they are very susceptible to heatstroke.

Confinement in a car is a leading cause of heatstroke. On a hot day, a car parked in the shade, with the windows partially open, can still reach temperatures exceeding 120°F (48.9°C) within a few minutes. Overexertion on a hot day can also cause heatstroke. Dogs that are heavily coated, old, or overweight are especially prone to heatstroke. What you consider a casual walk may be too much for your Pom on a hot day. Remember that for each of your steps, Charm has to take several rapid steps just to keep pace with you. In warm weather the temperature is much higher at pavement level than at your eye level. Because Charm is short, her entire underside is exposed

to a lot of heat as she walks on concrete or asphalt.

Signs of heatstroke include frantic, rapid breathing or struggling to breathe, panting, bright red gums and bright red curling tongue, thick drool, vomiting, diarrhea, dehydration, and a rectal temperature of 105 to 110°F (41 to 43°C). As the condition progresses, the body organs become affected, and the animal weakens, goes into shock and then a coma, and dies. All of this can happen in a very short period of time and death can occur rapidly.

If Charm is suffering from heatstroke, lower her body temperature immediately by repeatedly wetting her down with cool water. Do not use extremely cold water or ice water. If you cannot continually wet Charm down, then place her in a sink or tub filled with cool water. Keep her head above the water, especially if she is unconscious, so that she does not drown.

Check your Pom's body temperature every three minutes. Once the temperature has dropped to 102°F (39°C), stop wetting with cool water and monitor your pet closely. Do not try to give her water to drink until she is conscious, or she may aspirate the liquid into her lungs.

Heatstroke is a medical emergency. Even if Charm appears to be

You can give your Pom liquid medication or fluids by mouth using a syringe (without a needle) or an eye dropper. Place the tip of the syringe in the corner of your Pom's mouth, between the lips and slowly administer the fluid so she can easily swallow it. Don't squirt too much liquid too fast, or too far back in the throat, or your Pom could choke.

recovering, she will need lifesaving follow-up care at the veterinarian's, including intravenous fluids and various medications to treat shock and prevent cerebral edema (brain swelling), especially if her temperature reached 106°F (41.5°C) or more.

Hypoglycemia

Hypoglycemia (low blood sugar) is a common cause of death in young Pomeranians. Pom puppies are active and burn a lot of calories, so they should have food available at all times. After six months of age Poms may continue free feeding or eat meals scheduled every four to six hours, depending on weight and activity level. Adult Pomeranians may also develop hypoglycemia if they are stressed or fed only once daily. They cannot eat enough in one meal to provide the calories needed throughout the day.

Early signs of hypoglycemia may be subtle. The animal may simply sit quietly alone in a corner, but as blood sugar rapidly drops, symptoms quickly become more severe. Symptoms of hypoglycemia are drowsiness, lethargy, inactivity, weakness, odd behavior, pale gums, and nervous system signs such as lack of coordination, stumbling, and dilated pupils. If not treated immediately, the animal will have seizures and die.

Do not try to force food or liquid into Charm's mouth if she is unconscious. She can aspirate and choke to death. Instead, rub a sugar-rich substance on the gums, such as Nutrical (available from your veterinarian), or

Young Pom pups can suffer from hypothermia, low blood sugar, and dehydration. Keep your puppy safe, warm, well nourished, and well hydrated.

corn syrup. Hypoglycemia is often accompanied by hypothermia and dehydration. Wrap Charm in a blanket and keep her warm. Even if Charm seems to improve in a few minutes, she will need emergency follow-up care, so contact your veterinarian immediately.

Hypothermia

Pomeranian puppies are tiny and do not have much body fat. Do not be misled by all that fluffy puppy fur. Charm is smaller than she looks, and she can get cold very quickly. Very young Poms are particularly sensitive to the cold, and once they start to lose their body heat, they cannot regain it without help. Signs of hypothermia begin with shivering and progress to

Pomeranian Perils

The Three Deadly Dangers: Dehydration, Hypoglycemia, and Hypothermia

The Pomeranian's tiny size, high energy level, and fast metabolism make it challenging for this toy breed to stay hydrated, nourished, and warm. Compared with larger breeds, Poms have a greater body surface area to body mass ratio and a rapid metabolism. Put these factors together and they mean your Pom has more trouble retaining body heat and body moisture than bigger dogs, while she burns up calories more quickly.

Dehydration, hypoglycemia, and hypothermia work together as a deadly trio. Together they are the most common cause of death in small animals. Stressed, sick, very young, or very old Poms are especially at risk.

Treatment and prevention consist of fluid therapy (including balanced electrolytes), nourishment to keep blood sugar from falling too low, and keeping your Pom warm (not hot).

lethargy, slow heart rate, slow respiration, coma, and death.

Warm your Pom *slowly*! Rapid heating or overheating cause serious problems. Warm Charm by covering her body with a blanket. Leave her head exposed so you can watch her closely, and place her in a warm area. *Do not use an electric heating pad.* Instead, fill plastic water bottles with very warm (not hot!) water and wrap them in towels. Place the water bottles near, but not directly against, Charm's body. Contact your veterinarian immediately and continue to refill the bottles when they are no longer warm enough. Check Charm's body temperature every five minutes until it has returned to normal. Do not allow her temperature to rise above 101.5°F (39°C). Observe Charm closely for other signs of problems. She will need veterinary care, such as fluids and possibly intravenous dextrose (a kind of sugar), so take her to your veterinarian immediately.

Never feed a Pomeranian that is suffering from hypothermia. Wait until it is completely warmed.

Eye Injury

Eye injuries are extremely painful and should be treated immediately to relieve pain and increase the chances of saving the eye(s) and vision. Injured eyes are very sensitive to the light, so place your Pom in a dark room until you can contact your veterinarian. When transporting Charm to the hospital, place her in a travel crate and cover the crate with a blanket to keep it dark.

If the eyes require flushing and rinsing, use a commercial eyewash solution or saline solution intended for use in the eyes.

Insect Stings

Insect stings are a common cause of allergic reactions in Pomeranians. Because Poms will snap at flying insects, most stings occur in the mouth and throat, where you might not readily see them, or on the face. Insect stings also occur frequently on the front legs and feet. A severe allergic reaction can lead to facial and throat swelling, difficulty breathing, pain, lethargy, vomiting, and loss of consciousness.

Bees leave their stingers in the skin, but wasps and hornets do not. If a bee stings Charm, remove the stinger by gently scraping it in one direction with a small, stiff business card. If that does not work, remove the stinger with tweezers. Be gentle and try not to squeeze the stinger, or more venom will be injected into the site.

Apply a paste mixture of water and baking soda or an ice pack to the stung area to relieve pain. If the offending insect is a hornet or wasp, apply vinegar to the area for pain relief. You may also put a topical antihistamine cream around the stung area.

Some Poms develop a hypersensitivity and severe allergic reaction to insect stings that can lead to anaphylactic shock and death. If the swelling worsens, or if Charm becomes restless and has difficulty breathing, starts to vomit, develops diarrhea, or loses consciousness, contact your veterinarian immediately. This is a life-threatening situation, and immediate professional treatment is necessary. Sensitive animals can often benefit from antihistamines such as diphenhydramine (Benadryl) or chlorpheneramine.

Poisoning

Pomeranians can be poisoned by eating or inhaling toxic substances, or by contact with poisons on their skin, mucus membranes, or eyes. Signs of

Keep those beautiful eyes bright and clear. Eye injuries are painful and often more serious than they seem. If your Pom has an eye problem, contact your veterinarian immediately to prevent loss of sight or loss of the eye.

poisoning include restlessness, drooling, abdominal pain, vomiting, diarrhea, unconsciousness, seizures, shock, and death.

Common sources of backyard and garage poisonings are lawn fertilizers, weed killers, insecticides, chemically contaminated runoff water that has formed puddles in the yard, poisonous plants, rodent bait, and antifreeze (ethylene glycol). As mentioned earlier, there is a new type of antifreeze available that does not contain ethylene glycol and is considered nontoxic to pets.

Inside the house additional dangers lurk, including houseplants, medications, spoiled food, and chocolate.

If you know the source of Charm's poisoning, contact your veterinarian

Some types of medicines for humans are poisonous for dogs. Always check with your veterinarian before giving your Pom prescription medicine or home remedies.

The 10 Most Common Poisonings in Dogs

- Ibuprofen (Advil, Motrin)
- Chocolate
- Ant and roach baits
- Rodenticides (rat, mouse, gopher bait)
- Acetaminophen (Tylenol)
- Pseudoephedrine in cold medicines
- Thyroid hormones
- Bleach
- Fertilizer
- Hydrocarbons (found in paint, varnish, engine cleaners, furniture polish, lighter fluid)

immediately for advice. If the poison came in a container (for example, antifreeze or rodent poison), read the container label and follow the emergency instructions for treating poisoning. You can induce vomiting, when necessary, by giving 1/4 to 1/2 teaspoon (1–2 ml) of hydrogen peroxide 3 percent.

Activated charcoal is a good compound to use to dilute and adsorb ingested poisons. You can purchase activated charcoal in liquid, powder, or tablet form from your veterinarian or local pharmacy. Keep it in your first aid kit. If you do not have activated charcoal, and you do not have any products to induce vomiting, you can dilute the poison in Charm's gastrointestinal tract by giving her some milk. Do not try to give her any liquids or medication if she is unconscious.

The sooner the poisoning is diagnosed and treated, the better Charm's chances are for a full recovery. Poisonings require veterinary treatment in addition to the initial emergency care you provide. Contact your veterinarian immediately if you suspect Charm has been exposed to poison, even if you are not certain.

According to statistics gathered between 2001 and 2005 by the American Society for the Prevention of Cruelty to Animals (ASPCA) Animal Poison Control Center, the substances on the previous page are the ten most common causes of toxicoses in dogs.

Seizures

There are many causes of seizures, including trauma and poisoning. Epileptic seizures are believed to be inherited in some Pomeranian family lines. Seizures may be mild or severe, ranging from tremors of short duration, to violent convulsions, chomping jaws and frothing at the mouth, stiffening of the neck and limbs, and cessation of breathing. During a severe seizure, the animal is not conscious and can be hurt thrashing about on the floor. Charm may seem to be choking during a seizure, but avoid the temptation to handle her mouth, as you will be bitten. If her jaws clamp down on your fingers, they will not release until the seizure has ended. Simply try to prevent Charm from injuring herself or hitting her head during the seizure. After

Color Code for Gums

You can tell a lot about your Pomeranian's health just by checking the gums.
• Bright pink: normal
• Red: inflammation, fever, heatstroke, possible poisoning
• Red specks or red spots: bleeding problems or infection
• Pale pink or white: anemia, hemorrhage or significant blood loss
• Blue, gray: insufficient oxygen delivery to the body
• Yellow: jaundice (icterus), liver problems
• "Muddy": very serious, near death in some cases
• "Tacky" or sticky to the touch: dehydrated

a seizure, Charm will be exhausted and seem disoriented or dazed. Wrap her in a blanket to keep her comfortable, safe, and warm, and take her immediately to the doctor for emergency care.

Shock

Shock is a serious emergency condition in which there is a decreased blood supply to vital organs and the body tissues die. Blood loss, heatstroke, bacterial toxins, and severe allergic reactions all can cause an animal to go into shock.

Shock results in a rapid death unless immediate veterinary care—including fluid and oxygen therapy and a variety of medications—are provided. Signs of shock include vomiting, diarrhea, weakness, difficulty

One of the nicest things you can do for your aging Pom is to give her a soft, warm, comfortable, quiet place to rest.

breathing, increased heart rate, collapse, and coma.

Snake and Spider Bites

Your Pom can encounter danger in the house, backyard or garage, or on a camping trip. Signs of snake and spider bites include pain, swelling, darkened tissue coloration, and tissue death. Snake and spider bites require urgent care and antivenin (if available), antibiotics, and painkillers.

If a snake bites Charm, contact your veterinarian immediately. Most veterinarians who practice in areas where snakebites are common keep antivenin available. All dogs bitten by venomous snakes should be hospitalized and monitored for at least twenty-four hours.

Because of its tiny size, a Pomeranian cannot tolerate as large amounts of toxins as larger dogs. Your Pom can become seriously ill or die from a poisonous bite if she is not treated quickly.

The Senior Pom

Toy breeds live longer than larger breeds. With tender loving care and good nutrition, your Pomeranian may live for fifteen years or more. A Pomeranian is considered a senior citizen at seven years of age, although she might still act like a puppy! As Charm ages, you may begin to notice changes taking place in her behavior, activity level, and physical stature.

She may become arthritic, slow down, and sleep more. She may develop problems with urination or bowel movements. Pomeranians have a tendency to develop plaque and periodontal disease faster than many breeds, especially in their old age. Teeth and gums will need more attention and care because of rapid accumulation of plaque and tartar on the teeth. Some teeth may need to be extracted. Hair coat may become thinner, the skin less supple. Hearing and vision will diminish. These are all signs of the aging process.

As Charm's body ages, her metabolism may slow. Older Poms, especially those that have been neutered, have a tendency to gain weight. If your pet is overweight, she can suffer more from arthritis. Geriatric dogs can have weaker hearts, less efficient kidney and liver function, general muscle weakening and atrophy (shrinkage), and a gradual deterioration in condition with decreased resistance to diseases. Some Pomeranians have skin problems and hair loss in their later years, and others may show signs of senility. All of these are age-related changes. The rate at which they occur varies among Pomeranians and is influenced by genetics, nutrition, environment, and the quality of health care received in earlier years.

Old age is inevitable, but there are a lot of things you can do to keep Charm comfortable in her golden years.

When your Pom becomes a senior citizen, exercise should be limited to leisurely walks around the block. Make sure she has a clean, cozy bed on the return home.

1. Provide a soft, warm bed. Cold temperatures and hard surfaces are hard on old joints and make arthritis more painful.

2. Weigh Charm monthly to make sure she doesn't gain or lose too much weight.

3. Take Charm out daily for slow, easy, short walks on level, soft, non-slippery, surfaces and keep her toenails trimmed.

4. Do not allow your senior Pom to climb steep stairs or hills, jump on and off furniture, or walk on slippery surfaces. Carry Charm when she is tired.

5. Feed a diet formulated for senior dogs. Choose one that is right for Charm's age and health condition. An increase in protein quality has recently been shown to be beneficial for some geriatric dogs and to have anticancer and antidiabetes effects. Discuss protein requirements with your veterinarian. A high-protein diet may be hard on Charm if her kidneys or liver are not working well.

6. Schedule physical examinations for Charm every six months for early detection of age-related problems such as cataracts, dental disease, tumors, or organ failure. Charm may

need to have dental cleaning and polishing every six months. Older dogs are more sensitive to anesthesia, especially if they are overweight, so this is another good reason to monitor your Pom's weight.

7. If Charm has failing eyesight or is hard of hearing, try not to startle her. Speak to her reassuringly as you approach so she knows you are there. Be sure to caution children not to approach too quickly or loudly, so they are not bitten.

Euthanasia—When You Must Say Good-bye

The most difficult thing about owning and loving a pet is the knowledge that even with the very best of care, old age or illness, and eventually death, cannot be avoided. Because Pomeranians have a relatively long life span, you and your family will have developed a deep attachment to this canine family member over the years.

Just like adults, children have difficulty dealing with the death of a beloved pet. Loss of the family Pom may be the first loss a child experiences. Children are often as grief stricken, if not more so, than adults, so when considering euthanasia, it is very important to prepare children in the family for the loss in a compassionate manner appropriate for the children's ages and maturity levels. If handled skillfully, this sad time can give you an opportunity to discuss life, love, illness, and death, as well as address additional fears or concerns a child may have.

Euthanasia means putting an animal to death humanely, peacefully, and painlessly. For Pomeranians, euthanasia is usually done by first giving a sedative to make the animal sleep deeply, then placing a catheter in a vein and injecting a lethal substance that ends life painlessly and almost instantly.

Your veterinarian can help you find a pet cemetery or cremation service and answer any specific questions you have about euthanasia. *A good guide: If suffering cannot be relieved, or if the quality of life is poor, or if the bad days outnumber the good days, it is time to consider euthanasia.* You will make the right decision at the right time.

Take comfort in the knowledge that you took excellent care of your Pomeranian throughout her life and that you always made the best decisions about her health and welfare—even when you had to make the most difficult decision of all.

Pomeranian Predispositions: Special Health Concerns

Pomeranians, like all breeds, have certain medical conditions to which they are predisposed. This means that although the condition occurs in other breeds, it is seen more often in a particular breed. Some problems are inherited (genetic), and others may be congenital (the dog is born with the problem but is it not necessarily an inherited trait). Other types of problems may be acquired later in life.

The good news is that Pomeranians have very few medical problems compared to other toy breeds! Just because Pomeranians are predisposed to certain disorders does not mean that your Pom will ever experience any of them, but if she does, this list will help you recognize them.

Anal Sacs

• Impaction, infection, and abscesses: Signs are scooting and a foul-smelling discharge from the anus or perianal area; blood and pus may be present.

Eyes

• Entropion: defect caused by one or more of the eyelids rolling inward and irritating the surface of the eye by the lid and lashes rubbing on it. In Pomeranians, the lower eyelid is a problem more often than the upper eyelid. The eyelid usually turns inward starting at the inner corner of the eye. The condition is inherited and thought to be controlled by more than one gene, and affected puppies are born with the defect.

• Cataract: cloudiness of one or both lenses. Cataracts affect vision and can lead to blindness. Most cataracts in Pomeranians, except those caused by trauma or disease or other health problems, are believed to be hereditary.

• Progressive Retinal Atrophy (PRA): a disease of the visual cells of the retina. PRA eventually leads to blindness. In Pomeranians PRA is considered an autosomal recessive disease (both parents of the puppy must be a

Windows to the Soul

Your Pomeranian has beautiful, clear eyes that melt your heart. No wonder they are called "windows to the soul." Protect those fragile gems from injury, pain, and loss of vision. If you see your pet squinting or tearing, or if she has any discharge from the eyes, don't hesitate to contact your veterinarian immediately. Eye problems are serious and usually very painful and if not treated right away can cause permanent loss of vision.

Eye problems can occur at any stage of life and some conditions are hereditary.

Pomeranians should be examined annually by a board certified veterinary ophthalmologist and registered with the Canine Eye Registration Foundation.

carrier of the disease for the puppy to develop blindness).

Heart

• Patent ductus arteriosus (PDA): While a fetus is developing, there is a normal connection (ductus) between the pulmonary artery and the aorta. This ductus closes shortly after birth. If it does not, blood from the high-pressure left side of the heart is forced into the pulmonary artery, causing pulmonary (lung) hypertension and eventually heart damage and cardiovascular collapse. Surgery is the only method for correcting the problem. Among the list of breeds affected by PDA, Pomeranians rank near the top.

The condition is believed to be inherited in Pomeranians and probably controlled by several genes.

Nervous System
• Epilepsy and seizures: considered to be hereditary in many cases.

Reproductive
• Cryptorchidism: one or both testicles retained in the abdominal cavity or inguinal ring. Testicles are usually descended by six weeks of age, although Pomeranian testicles may be too small to easily find at that age. Retained testes should be surgically removed or they can develop Sertoli cell tumors later in life. In cryptorchid Pomeranians, the right testicle is most frequently retained.
• Dystocia: difficulty delivering puppies. Pomeranians usually have small litters and often require surgery to deliver their puppies because Pomeranian puppies have large heads in relation to the size of the birth canal.

Respiratory
• Tracheal collapse: a flattening of the tracheal rings causing a reduction in the diameter of the trachea. It is common in Pomeranians and may be congenital. Several causes have been suggested, including cartilage defect. Signs are observed at an early age and usually follow activity, play, or excitement. A characteristic "goose honk" cough is frequently noted. Retching and fainting can also occur. Obesity, heart disease, and bronchitis worsen the condition. Treatment consists of rest, stress reduction, possible surgery, and a wide selection of medications (corticosteroids, antibiotics, bronchodilators), and weight reduction if needed.

Skeletal
• Patellar luxation: the kneecap slips in and out of proper position because of a flaw in bone (femur) structure and weak ligaments. When the kneecap slips, the lower rear leg seems to lock and the Pom moves with a skipping or hopping gait. The skipping continues until the knee slips back into its groove. The condition occurs at a young age and tends to worsen with growth and age. Patellar luxation is graded from 1 to 4, with 4 being the most severe case. Mild patellar luxation (grade 1) may not require surgery, but grades 2, 3, and 4 must be corrected surgically to prevent pain, lameness, and degenerative joint disease. It is common in Pomeranians.
• Dwarfism: Some genetic lines of Pomeranians produce "dwarfs," also called *teacups* or *munchkins*. Dwarf Pomeranians usually have health problems, and these dogs should not be used for breeding.
• Hydrocephalus: caused by cerebrospinal fluid (CSF) buildup in the ventricles (spaces) of the brain, resulting in compression and brain damage. Signs include a domed head, open fontanelles, seizures, visual problems, and learning impairment.

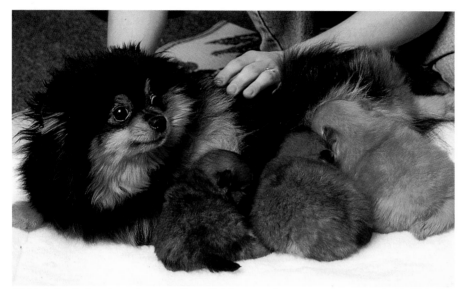

Think twice before breeding your Pom. Raising puppies is hard work for the mother— and for you. Be prepared for possible medical bills and health risks for the mother and pups. Some Poms require an emergency cesarian section.

• Open fontanelles: "soft spots" on the skull caused by failure of bones in the skull to close.

Skin Problems

• Alopecia: hair loss.
  – Fleas and allergies to fleas
  – Skin infections
  – Food allergies: often with hair loss around head and neck
  – Allergies to environment (pollen, dust mites, grass, carpet, yard)
  – Autoimmune diseases
  – Hormonal (endocrine) imbalance: hypothyroidism and growth hormone dermatosis
    ◦ Sex hormone dermatosis alopecia X is a major cause of hair loss in Pomeranians. It is also known as hair cycle arrest, alopecia X, black skin disease, adult-onset growth hormone deficiency, hyposomatotropism, and castration-responsive alopecia. Signs include symmetrical hair loss from both sides of the body, neck, and tail and darkened skin. Studies suggest the problem is caused by a genetically sex-linked deficiency of growth hormone.

Teeth

• Abnormal placement of teeth: misalignment, malocclusion
• Abnormal number of teeth: missing teeth, retained deciduous (baby) teeth
• Dental and periodontal disease: excessive accumulation of plaque and tartar on the teeth and gum inflammation. If not treated, the bacteria in the gums can spread through the bloodstream, grow on heart valves, and form abscesses in the kidneys and liver.

Chapter Ten

The Performance Pomeranian: Training Your Pom

From the moment you bring him home, your Pomeranian puppy will start learning lessons that will shape his life. With your training and guidance, Max will learn the basic commands: *come, sit, down, stand, stay,* and *heel.* He will learn to be well mannered and obedient. Pomeranians are highly intelligent and eager to please, so how far you go beyond the basics will depend entirely on how much time you spend with Max. Training is fun. Do not be surprised if you are bitten by the training bug and the two of you later become competitive team members in the agility or obedience rings. With a Pomeranian, anything is possible!

Basic commands such as *sit, down,* and *stand* are best taught on a tabletop. This gives you the advantage of not having to bend or stoop or sit on the floor while working with your tiny companion. It also gives you more control over your pet because when he is on the tabletop, he really has fewer distractions and nowhere to run. All of his attention will be focused on you and you can work comfortably. The most important thing to remember is to never leave your Pom unattended on the table.

The best way to keep Max's attention is to keep training sessions short, make them fun and interesting, and always end on a positive note. Lots of praise and a small food reward are the best incentives for your Pom to learn quickly and do the right thing. Later, praise him every time he does something right and give him a food reward sometimes, but not every time. By keeping Max guessing when the treat is coming, you will keep his attention longer.

The Basics

Teaching your Pom the basic commands—*sit, down,* and *stand*—have been previously discussed in detail (see "Grooming Your Pomeranian"), using a tabletop. Teaching Max to come, stay, and heel must be taught at ground level.

Stay is one of the most important commands to teach your Pom. It could also save his life.

Come

Max first must learn his name so he knows who he is and so you can get his attention. Start by calling his name when you feed him and using his name when you play with him. It will not take Max long to associate his name with fun and food.

Start by sitting or standing a short distance away from your pet. Let him see that you have a small food reward. Enthusiastically say, "Max, come!" As soon as he comes to you, give him the food reward and lots of praise. You can also make this into a game, saying, "Max, come!" while moving away from him, making him have to travel more distance to meet you. As you increase the distance, you will need to have an assistant hold Max until you move away from him and restrain him until you give the command to come;

otherwise he may leave his spot and follow you before you can call him.

Over time you can decrease the frequency of food rewards, but always continue the praise. In a short time Max will learn to come when called, and he will do it purely for the attention you bestow on him, but that does not mean you cannot continue to surprise him with a food reward now and then!

Stay

Stay is a tough command for Pomeranians, because they want to be in the middle of all activities and are constantly in motion. Asking Max to stay somewhere else while you walk away will upset him. He will try to follow you because he does not want to be left behind. Pomeranians are very sensitive. Your Pom's feelings

where he is. It will not make sense to him in the beginning.

Stay is an important command that Max should learn. It can come in handy in emergency situations. Be patient and work in small steps. Little by little Max will understand what you want him to do.

To avoid injury, do not teach Max this command on the tabletop. He will not always obey your stay *command and might jump off the table and be injured.*

To teach Max to stay, make him sit. Then show him the palm of your hand and say, "Stay." Learning the *stay* command is the one time you will not use your Pom's name to get his attention, because if you do, he may think that you want him to come to you. Take two or three steps away from Max. If he gets up to follow, return him to the same location and say, "Max, sit." After he sits, show him the palm of your hand again, say "stay," and take a few steps back. For the first few training sessions, if Max remains in place for ten to fifteen seconds, he deserves lots of praise. Let Max know when it is all right to get up by using the same release word(s) every time, such as "O.K.", or "good boy." If Max is still for thirty seconds, a food reward is in order! As you repeat these lessons and as Max gets older and more patient, you can gradually extend the stay periods to a few minutes. It will not take long for Max to associate your hand signal and the

may be hurt if you are too harsh when you tell him to stay. In the beginning, Max should be expected to stay in place only for a very short time period.

Do not try to teach Max to stay until he has learned the *come, sit,* and *down* commands very well. This is important so you do not undo the successful training you have already accomplished. At first Max will be confused by your command because for most of his early training you have been asking him to come to you. Now you are going to ask him to remain

Never call your Pomeranian for purposes of disciplining him if he misbehaves. He will not associate the reprimand with his bad deed and will be confused. He will think you scolded him for coming to you when called. Always praise your Pom when he comes when called.

word *stay* with being asked to remain in place.

Leash Training

Studies have shown that leash training is easiest if started when a puppy is five to nine weeks of age. Leash training actually begins without a leash. It starts with the simple process of encouraging your puppy to follow you around the house or yard and to come when called. Once these simple goals are accomplished, you can begin by attaching a light line, such as a piece of yarn or string, to your Pom's collar and letting him drag it behind him. Encourage Max to follow you with the string dangling along. When Max has become accustomed to the string, replace it with a very thin, light leash called a show lead. You can purchase one of these from the many online dog product suppliers or at a dog show.

Max will quickly adapt to the show lead dragging on the ground behind him, and when he has, you can pick it up and walk with him. Hold the lead and follow Max wherever he goes. Do not pull or tug on the lead. This way Max will not be bothered by the lead or struggle against it. He probably will ignore it. Never pull on the lead or you can injure your Pom's delicate throat or trachea (windpipe). Poms are predisposed to tracheal collapse, and pulling on your pet's collar and neck could worsen the condition or damage your pet's trachea. Some Poms do better in their early training if a harness is used instead of a collar.

Never leave your Pom alone, not even for a moment, when he has yarn, string, or a show lead attached to his collar or harness.

With each new training session, begin to gently guide your pet—not by his neck, but by continually encouraging him to walk with you and offering him food rewards. Be patient, enthusiastic, and consistent. Start with short distances, across the living room or across part of the backyard. If Max does not want to come along, simply stop where you are and wait. Do not drag him or pull on his neck. Do not let Max struggle against the lead. As long as Max follows you, or stays close to you, give him a food reward.

With patience and lots of praise, Max will soon be following along on the lead. He may weave a bit, or run a little ahead, or drop behind for a moment to investigate something interesting on the ground, but he will have the general idea. Once he reaches this level in training, you can begin to work on fine-tuning him to heel.

Heel

Stand with your Pomeranian on your left side and continue to use food rewards to encourage him to walk with you. If your Pom has a favorite spot in the house or backyard, walk to that spot together, always keeping Max on your left side. Be careful not to trip over or step on your Pom—it is easy to do!

When Max has learned to stay on your left side and keep pace with you,

Use a light lead and a comfortable collar when you train your Pom to heel.

it is time to teach him to sit when you stop walking. He should already know the *sit* command very well. When he sits, give him a food reward and lots of praise. When you are ready to resume your walk, say his name and then the command "*Heel*" and step out with your left foot at the same time. Max should jump up to follow; when he does, praise him and give him a treat. Repeat the exercise, walking a little bit farther each time and asking Max to sit at your left side each time you stop. Pomeranians are quick learners. If you make the training session seem more like a game, your Pom will be eager to participate and to please. In no time at all you will both be taking leisurely strolls throughout the neighborhood, enjoying every step of the way!

Top of the Class

Dog training classes are a lot of fun. They are rewarding not only because your Pom becomes a model citizen and a wonderful ambassador for his breed, but because you also will form many lasting friendships.

Pomeranians are exceptionally bright dogs, capable of learning just about anything, as long as they have a good trainer that they trust. A basic puppy class, or dog training class, is one of the most fun and effective ways to train your Pom. Keep in mind that there are as many different training techniques as there are dogs and trainers. When considering a dog training class, it is a good idea to sit in on a few sessions in the beginning to make sure the trainer's style and techniques will work for you and Max.

Training should always be enjoyable for you and your Pom. Pomeranians are showoffs that love games and activities. As Max graduates from each training level, you may well find him at the top of his class. Your performing Pom may be an excellent candidate for the obedience and agility rings. With all that training, you suddenly realize this is only the beginning! When it comes to dog competitions, there is no finish line!

Chapter Eleven

Poms with a Purpose: Competition, Conformation, Companionship

Tracking

Pomeranians have an excellent sense of smell. Make an interesting game for Max by hiding little tidbits of his favorite food around the house and yard for him to find. Make the game more complicated by hiding the treats one to two hours in advance of the search and increasing the distance between treats. If Max has a natural ability for this game, consider contacting the American Kennel Club for a Tracking Regulations brochure. Max may be a gifted candidate, capable of earning a Tracking Dog title!

Agility: License to Thrill!

Agility competitions are exciting, fast-paced, timed events in which dogs complete challenging obstacle courses, jump over objects, teeter on seesaws, walk planks, run through tunnels, jump through hoops, and weave in and out between poles. Titles that can be earned, in increasing level of difficulty, are Novice Agility (NA), Open Agility (OA), Agility Excellent (AX), and Master Agility Excellent (MX).

This competitive Pom proves he is a pro as he thrills his admirers and shows that Poms can do it all!

If you plan on participating in dog events, take your Pom to the shows from the time he is young. The socialization and exposure will prepare him for future competitions.

Pomeranians that love agility are keen competitors. They do not know that they are tiny. They see themselves as big and powerful as their Wolfspitzen ancestors. In your Pom's mind, no obstacle or course is too large or difficult. All he asks is the opportunity to get out there and show everyone what he can do.

Preparation for the agility course includes advanced training sessions and lots of strengthening and conditioning exercises. After all, as an agility dog, your tiny toy is an athlete in the truest sense of the word.

Obedience Trials

Pomeranians have it all—beauty *and* brains. It is no surprise that Pomeranians do as well in obedience trials as they do in the conformation ring. In obedience trials, it is intelligence that counts. Dogs are put through a series of exercises and commands and judged according to how well they perform. Each dog starts out with 200 points. Points are subtracted throughout the trials or tests for lack of attention, nonperformance, barking, or slowness.

Obedience trials are divided into three levels that are progressively more difficult and challenging: Novice—Companion Dog (C.D.), Open—Companion Dog Excellent (C.D.X.), and Utility—Utility Dog (U.D.).

To earn a C.D. title, the dog must be able to perform six exercises: heel on leash, stand for examination, heel free, recall, long sit, and long down. To earn a C.D.X. title the dog must be able to heel free, drop on recall, retrieve on flat, retrieve over the high jump, broad jump, long sit, and long down. To earn a U.D., the dog must be able to respond to signal exercise, scent discrimination tests, directed retrieve, directed jumping, and group examination. The dog must earn three legs to receive its title. To receive a leg the dog must earn at least 170 points out of a possible perfect score of 200 and receive more than 50 percent on each exercise.

Fun Matches

You can prepare yourself and your puppy for a future in the conformation ring by attending fun matches. Fun matches are just that—fun! They are hosted by American Kennel Club (AKC) approved breed clubs and are conducted according to American Kennel Club show rules. Only pure-bred, AKC-registered dogs may participate. However, fun matches do not count toward points for a championship, and dogs that have won points toward a championship do not compete. Judges at fun matches may be official AKC judges or knowledge-able dog breeders or handlers selected by the hosting club. Fun matches are a great way for you and your puppy to practice all aspects of a real dog show, from traveling to grooming, to exhibiting, to winning!

Conformation Show Ring

In conformation classes, Pomeranians are judged on how closely they come to the ideal standard for their breed. If Max is handsome enough to

Poms are exceptionally bright and highly motivated. The more you train your Pom, the more he can do, and the more fun you both will have.

compete against the best of his breed, consider joining a Pomeranian club, as well as a local kennel club. These clubs can provide you with information on show dates and locations, judges, professional handlers and canine activities, and even offer handling classes to teach you and your Pom the ropes.

Specialty Shows

Under AKC show regulations, there are specialty and group shows, and all-breed shows. Dogs are judged according to their breed standard and, by process of elimination, one dog is selected as Best of Breed.

For some Pom aficionados, the only thing more fun than having one Pomeranian is having two Pomeranians!

A specialty show is limited to a designated breed or grouping of breeds. The show is held under AKC rules and held by the individual breed clubs, in this case, the American Pomeranian Club (APC).

To become a champion, a Pomeranian must win points by competing in formal American Kennel Club sanctioned, licensed events. The points must be accumulated as major wins under different judges.

All-Breed Shows

As the name implies, all-breed shows are for all breeds. Judging is conducted according to AKC rules. In addition to Best of Breed winners, open shows offer the titles of Best in Group (for dogs considered to be the best representative of their group) and Best in Show (for the dog selected as the best representative of its breed and group, compared with all other dogs of other breeds and groups).

Most dogs competing in specialty or open shows are competing for points toward their championship. A dog can earn from one to five points at a show. The number of points available depends upon the number of entries. Wins of three, four, or five points are called "majors." The fifteen points required for a championship title must be won under at least three different judges and include two majors won under two different judges.

There are five different classes in which a dog can compete for championship points and the classes are divided by sex:

Puppy class (divided into six–nine months of age and nine–twelve months of age)

Novice

Bred by exhibitor

American bred

Open

Male dogs are judged first, in this order: Puppy dogs, Novice dogs, Bred by exhibitor dogs, American bred dogs, and Open dogs. The first-place winners in each class later return to the ring to compete against each other. This class is called the Winners Class. The dog selected as the best male in the Winners Class is the Winners Dog. This is the dog that will win the championship points in the show. The male that placed second to the Winners Dog that was in the Winners Dog's original class (Puppy, Novice, Bred by exhibitor, American bred, or Open) is then brought in to join the Winners Class to compete against the remaining four dogs in the class. The dog that wins second place in the Winners Class is the Reserve Winners Dog. If, for any reason, the AKC disallows the championship points to the Winners Dog, the Reserve Winners Dog will receive the points. The same procedure is then followed, in the same order, for the females, and the Winners Bitch, who also wins championship points, and Reserve Winners Bitch are selected.

The Winners Dog and Winners Bitch then compete in a class called the Best of Breed. Entered in this class are dogs and bitches that already have won their championship titles.

If your Pom is a good candidate for the show ring, give it a try. Your Pom will love to show off as much as you will love showing him—and you just might win!

The judge selects either the Winners Dog or the Winners Bitch to be Best of Winners. Then the judge selects an animal from the group to be Best of Breed. If the Best of Breed winner is a male, the judge selects the best bitch to be Best of Opposite Sex to the Best of Winners. If the Best of Breed winner is a female, the judge selects a male for Best of Opposite Sex to the Best of Winners.

At an all-breed show, judging takes place for each breed and each Best of Breed winner competes in its breed group. The first-place winners of each breed group then compete against each other for the coveted title of Best in Show.

At Your Service: The Pomeranian Companion, Protector, and Service Dog

Pomeranians are wonderful companions. They form strong bonds with their owners, are very protective of them, and make excellent watchdogs. Poms are also talented service and therapy dogs. Whether saving lives, or simply enriching lives, busy Pomeranians work their magic in countless ways every day.

Breaking the Sound Barrier

Pomeranians make excellent hearing dogs. Pomeranians are taught in special training centers to serve as ears for owners with hearing impairments. Poms learn to run to the source of the sound (such as a fire alarm, doorbell, knock, person's voice, oven timer, smoke alarm, telephone, carbon monoxide monitor alarm, running water, and alarm clocks) back to their owners and back again to the sound. In this way Pomeranians alert their owners to possible dangers and make it possible for people to be more independent and feel more secure.

Therapy Dog Extraordinaire

Nothing brightens the day more than a smile—especially a Pomeranian smile! Many societies specialize in training Pomeranians to serve as pet-facilitated therapy dogs for adult day-care centers and health-care facilities. A well-mannered, well-trained, plush, petit Pom can play a big role in bringing happiness and affection to the lives of many patients. Poms fit any lap and every heart!

The Quintessential Canine

From the icy terrains of Lapland and Iceland, to the province of Pomerania,

Poms leave indelible footprints in the hearts of their admirers!

across the sea to the queen's palace, and across the ocean into your living room, and onto your lap—the Pomeranian has come a long, long way. Whether Best in Show or best friend, your Pom is a natural winner! He has charmed admirers around the globe and ranks among the most popular breeds in the world. This tiny Spitz with the giant heart has proven that he can do just about anything and exceed your expectations. Give him the care, love, and training he deserves and let him surprise you!

Information

Kennel and Breed Clubs

American Pomeranian Club, Inc.
National Breeder Referral
Jane Lehtinen (218) 741-2117
Brenda Turner, Secretary
3910 Concord Place
Texarkana, TX 75501-2212
www.americanpomeranianclub.org

American Kennel Club (AKC)
Registrations
5580 Centerview Drive
Raleigh, NC 27606-3390
(919) 233-9767
www.akc.org

The Canadian Kennel Club
89 Skyway Avenue, Suite 100
Etobicoke, Ontario M9W 6R4
Canada
(416) 675-5511
www.ckc.ca

Federation Cynologique Internationale
Secretariat General de la FCA
Place Albert 1er, 13
B-6530 Thuin, Belgium
www.fci.be/english

The Kennel Club
1-4 Clargis Street, Picadilly
London W7Y 8AB England
www.the-kennel-club.org.uk

States Kennel Club
1007 W. Pine Street
Hattiesburg, MS 39401
(601) 583-8345

United Kennel Club (UKC)
100 East Kilgore Road
Kalamazoo, MI 49001-5598
(616) 343-9020
www.ukcdogs.com

North American Dog Agility Council
P.O. Box 277
St. Maries, ID 83861
(208) 689-3803

United States Dog Agility Association
P.O. Box 850955
Richardson, TX 75085-8955
(972) 231-9700
Fax: (214) 503-0161
E-mail: *info@usdaa.com*
www.usdaa.com

Health-related Associations and Foundations

AKC Canine Health Foundation
251 W. Garfield Road
Aurora, OH 44202
(216) 995-0806
E-mail: *akchf@aol.com*

American Society for the Prevention
of Cruelty to Animals (ASPCA)
424 East 92nd Street
New York, NY 10128-6804
(212) 876-7700
www.aspca.org

American Veterinary Medical
Association (AVMA)
930 North Meacham Road
Schaumberg, IL 60173
www.avma.org

Canine Eye Registration Foundation
(CERF)
South Campus Court, Building C
West Lafayette, IN 47907
www.vmdb.org/cerf.html

Delta Society
289 Perimeter Road E.
Renton, WA 98055
(800) 869-6898
www.deltasociety@cis.
compuserve.com

Dogs for the Deaf
10175 Wheeler Road
Central Point, OR 97502
(541) 826-9220
E-mail: *info@dogsforthedeaf.org*
www.dogsforthedeaf.org

San Francisco S.P.C.A. Hearing
Dogs Program
2500 16th Street
San Francisco, CA 94103
(415) 554-3020
E-mail: *hearingdog@sfspca.org*
www.hearingdog.com
www.sfspca.org

A beautiful Pomeranian will steal the
show and steal your heart!

National Education for Assistance
Dog Services
P.O. Box 213
West Boylston, MA 01583
(508) 422-9064
www.neads.org

Therapy Dogs Inc.
P.O. Box 2786
Cheyenne, WY 82003
(307) 638-3223
www.therapydogs.com

Therapy Dogs International
719 Daria Lane
Fallbrook, CA 92028-1505
www.tdi@gti.net

Institute for Genetic Disease
in Animals
P.O. Box 222
Davis, CA 97617
www.vetmed.ucdavis.edu/gdc/gdc.htm

International Canine Semen Bank
P.O. Box 651
Sandy, OR 97055
(503) 663-7031
www.ik9sb.com

International Canine Semen
   Bank—San Diego
P.O. Box 668
Lakeside, CA 92040
(619) 654-4520
www.sharonvanderlip.com

National Animal Poison Control
   Center (NAPCC)
Animal Product Safety Service
1717 South Philo Road, Suite 36
Urbana, IL 61802
(888) 4ANI-HELP
(888) 426-4435
(900) 680-0000
www.napcc.aspca.org

Orthopedic Foundation for Animals
   (OFA)
2300 Nifong Boulevard
Columbia, MO 65201
www.prodogs.com

Lost Pet Registries

The American Kennel Club (AKC)
AKC Companion Recovery
5580 Centerview Drive, Suite 250
Raleigh, NC 27606-3394
(800) 252-7894
E-mail: *found@akc.org*
www.akc.org/car.htm

AVID Microchip
(800) 336-AVID
E-mail: *pettrac@aol.com*

Home Again Microchip Service
(800) LONELY-ONE
www.homeagainpets.com

National Dog Registry (NDR)
P.O. Box 118
Woodstock, NY 12498-0116
(800) 637-3647
www.nationaldogregistry.com

Petfinders
368 High Street
Athol, NY 12810
(800) 223-4747
www.petclub.org

Your Pom is a precious gift of nature, with a mystical smile, and wrapped in a beautiful coat!

Periodicals

The American Kennel Club Gazette
51 Madison Avenue
New York, NY 10010
www.akc.org

Dog Fancy
Subscription Division
P.O. Box 53264
Boulder, CO 80323-3264
(303) 786-7306/666-8504
www.dogfancy.com

Dogs USA Annual
P.O. Box 55811
Boulder, CO 80322-5811
(303) 786-7652

Dog World
29 North Wacker Drive
Chicago, IL 60606
(312) 726-2802

Books

The Complete Dog Book, Official Publication of the American Kennel Club. New York: Howell Book House, 1992.

Cawthera, Averil. *Living with a Pomeranian.* Hauppauge, NY: Barron's Educational Series, Inc. 2003.

Cunliffe, Juliette. *Pomeranian.* Allenhurst, NJ: Kennel Club Books, LLC. 2004.

Moreno, Julie. *A New Owner's Guide to Pomeranians.* Neptune City, NJ: T.F.H. Publications, Inc. 2003.

Stahlkuppe, Joe. *Pomeranians: A Complete Pet Owner's Manual.* Hauppauge, NY: Barron's Educational Series, Inc. 2000.

Vanderlip, Sharon and Ludwig, Gert. *1000 Dog Names from A to Z.* Hauppauge, NY: Barron's Educational Series, Inc. 2005.

Index